H.W.Brewer

The City Centre as it would have looked in 1889.

BIRMINGHAM REMEMBERED

Alton Douglas
Dennis Moore

additional research by Jo Douglas

Published by Brewin Books, Doric House, Church Street, Studley, Warks. B80 7LG.

Printed by WASP Litho Ltd.

4th Impression

ISBN 0 947731 95 4

CONTENTS

4 INTRODUCTION

6 ROYAL OCCASIONS

13 BIRMINGHAM AT ARMS

19 MADE AND SOLD IN BIRMINGHAM

32 SMITHFIELD MARKET

33 SPORT

41 ENTERTAINING THE CITY

57 EVENTS

79 THE HUB OF THE WHEEL

109 HERE AND THERE

135 ACKNOWLEDGEMENTS

136 ALTON'S OTHER BOOKS

THE LORD MAYOR'S PARLOUR,

THE COUNCIL HOUSE,

BIRMINGHAM, B1 1BB.

As Lord Mayor of Birmingham, in its 100th year as a City, I am delighted to see the publication of "Birmingham Remembered". It reminds me of the great changes that have taken place during my lifetime in Birmingham and, most importantly, it illustrates the progress that has been made through the energy and enterprise of the people of this great City of ours over the last 100 years. We can now look forward with confidence to another century of growth, vitality and achievement.

Harold Blumenthal.

INTRODUCTION

by Patrick C. Baird, B.A., A.L.A., Head of Local Studies Dept., Birmingham Central Library.

Birmingham is now the premier provincial city in the United Kingdom, and a renowned industrial city, but the origins of its prosperity, in trade and manufacturing, date back to the Middle Ages. Royal recognition of this came in 1166 when Henry II gave the Lord of the Manor, Peter de Bermingham, a charter to hold a market and later in 1250 when William de Bermingham was granted permission by Henry III to hold a fair for merchants.

Birmingham's importance as a centre for craftsmen was firmly established by 1327 and by 1500 the smiths of Birmingham were selling their wares throughout England, including London. One sixteenth-century writer, William Camden, noted in his book "Britannia" (in 1563) "I went to Birmingham swarming with inhabitants and echoing with the noise of anvils, for here are a great number of smiths. The lower part (probably Deritend) is very wet. The upper part (the Bull Ring) is adorned with handsome buildings".

During the Civil War in the 1640's Birmingham supplied swords, pikes and armour principally to the Parliamentary forces, although some say that the King's troops were also using implements of war manufactured in Birmingham. However, the area still emerged from this war with its reputation enhanced.

In 1690 Alexander Missen in his "Travels" boasted that he saw at Milan "fine works of rock crystal, swords, heads for canes, snuff boxes and other fine works of steel; but they can be had better and cheaper at Birmingham".

It was also at this time that Birmingham became involved in gun manufacture and in 1690 the government, requiring arms to use in skirmishes with France and Ireland, placed contracts with Birmingham workers to supply 200 muzzle-loading muskets a month. By 1754 one Birmingham firm alone was exporting 600 weapons per week. The eighteenth century saw Birmingham make the most rapid strides in its history. It became the industrial, commercial and cultural capital of the Midlands and became a centre for freethinking men of ideas - people such as the printer John Baskerville; Joseph Priestley, who, amongst other scientific achievements, discovered the elements of oxygen; William Withering, who popularised digitalis as a remedy for heart disease; William Murdoch, inventor of gas lighting; James Watt, who developed the steam engine, and Matthew Boulton, the eminent industrialist. Boulton's Soho factory, which by the end of the eighteenth century employed more men than any other in the continent of Europe, was the first to be lit by gas to allow production to take place at night.

Commerce grew alongside this increased industrial wealth. Two of the country's well-known "clearing banks", Lloyds and The Midland, were founded in Birmingham, and it has also been claimed that the world's first building society was established in the developing town.

By 1800 Birmingham was booming, and after the Reform Act of 1832 was created a parliamentary borough. Nevertheless, it had not yet received a municipal charter so could not officially be recognised as a town. Steps were eventually taken in March 1837, to obtain the important charter, and on 6th March 1838, "The Birmingham Journal" announced that Queen Victoria had granted the Charter of Incorporation which meant that Birmingham was now legally "a town", with the first Town Council being elected on Wednesday, 26th December 1838. A few weeks prior to this it is recorded that the town charter was sent from London by train on the newly-opened London to Birmingham railway, but was mislaid and later found in Belfast. Fifty years later, on 4th December 1888, the Town Council sent a petition to Queen Victoria expressing the wish that as the Corporation had now completed fifty years of municipal life, and as Birmingham was the largest borough in the country that had not yet received the title of "City", it hoped that this would be conferred upon the borough. The petition was promptly granted by the Queen and the Letters Patent under the Great Seal acknowledging the status of "City" were issued without pomp or ceremony on 14th January 1889.

THE MAYOR:—That will look a bit better, Mr. Smith!
THE TOWN CLERK:—Yes, and perhaps the council will remember that
 I am a City Clerk now—My salary might be—
THE MAYOR:—Oh! Ah! Um!

7th DEC. 1888.

Richard Cadbury Barrow, Mayor, 1888/9.

1889, February 6: At the first
meeting of the City Council
the Mayor (Ald. Barrow)
announced the receipt of the
Royal Charter constituting
Birmingham a city.

DESCRIPTION OF THE ARMS AND SUPPORTERS

Granted to the Corporation, April 1889

ARMS

Quarterly First and Fourth Azure a Bend of five Lozenges Or, second and third per pale indented of the last and Gules, over all a Fesse Ermine thereon a Mural Crown of the second. And for the Crest, on a wreath of the Colours A Mural Crown, issuant therefrom a dexter Arm embowed the hand holding a hammer all proper, the Motto "Forward."

SUPPORTERS

On the dexter side A Man habited as a Smith (representing Industry) holding in the dexter hand a Hammer resting on an Anvil all proper And on the sinister side A Female Figure (representing Art) proper vested Argent wreathed round the temples with Laurel Vert tied by a Riband Gules holding in the dexter hand resting on the Shield a Book bound also Gules and in the sinister a Painter's Palette Or with two Brushes proper.

5

ROYAL OCCASIONS

Since that memorable day on 14th January 1889 every British ruling monarch has visited the city and there have been princes, princesses, dukes and duchesses here too. Only Edward VIII, later the Duke of Windsor, never came here as King. His visits were as the Prince of Wales.

Royal visits are marked by foundation stones around the city and by hospitals, schools, streets, roads, halls and centres which bear their names.

Everywhere they have been, royalty has received a warm response and affection. To gain a better view of them small boys have shinned up drainpipes and men have climbed trees and street-lamps. Schoolchildren, dodging under the cordon of police, have pressed posies and presents on their favourite prince or princess. Mayors and civic dignitaries, joining in the processions or "walk-abouts", have been captured on film by hundreds of cameras held by jostled, amateur photographers. Some particularly fortunate people have even managed a royal handshake or received a friendly word.

Opening of the Birmingham Technical School, Suffolk Street, (later renamed the Matthew Boulton Technical College) by the Duke of Devonshire, 13th December 1895. This is a composite photograph as the four dignitaries on the left were added later.

King Edward VII and Queen Alexandra arrive to inaugurate the Elan Valley Water Scheme for Birmingham, 21st July 1904.

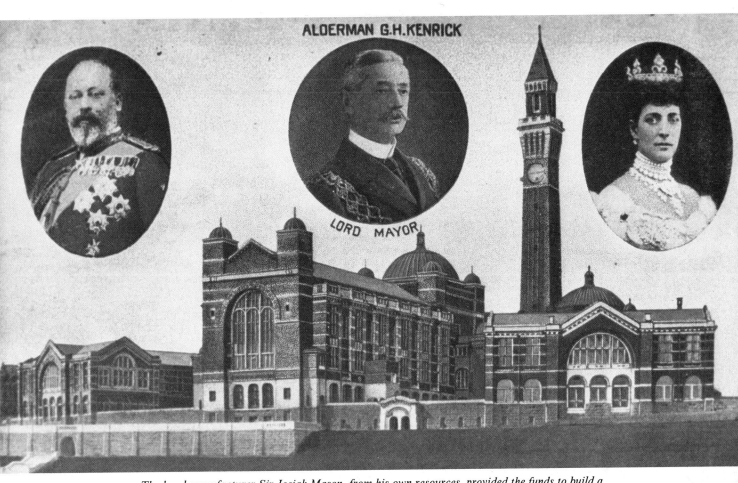

ALDERMAN G.H. KENRICK

LORD MAYOR

The local manufacturer Sir Josiah Mason, from his own resources, provided the funds to build a science college named after him in Edmund Street. Joined by the Birmingham School of Medicine and Surgery in 1892, this led to the creation by Royal Charter in 1900, of the University at Bournbrook. By 7th July 1909 sufficient buildings were ready for the official opening by King Edward VII and Queen Alexandra. Mason College was demolished in 1963 to make way for the new Reference and Central Lending Library.

King George V and Queen Mary, with Mr and Mrs George Cadbury, visit the almshouses, Linden Road/Maryvale Road, Bournville, 22nd May 1919.

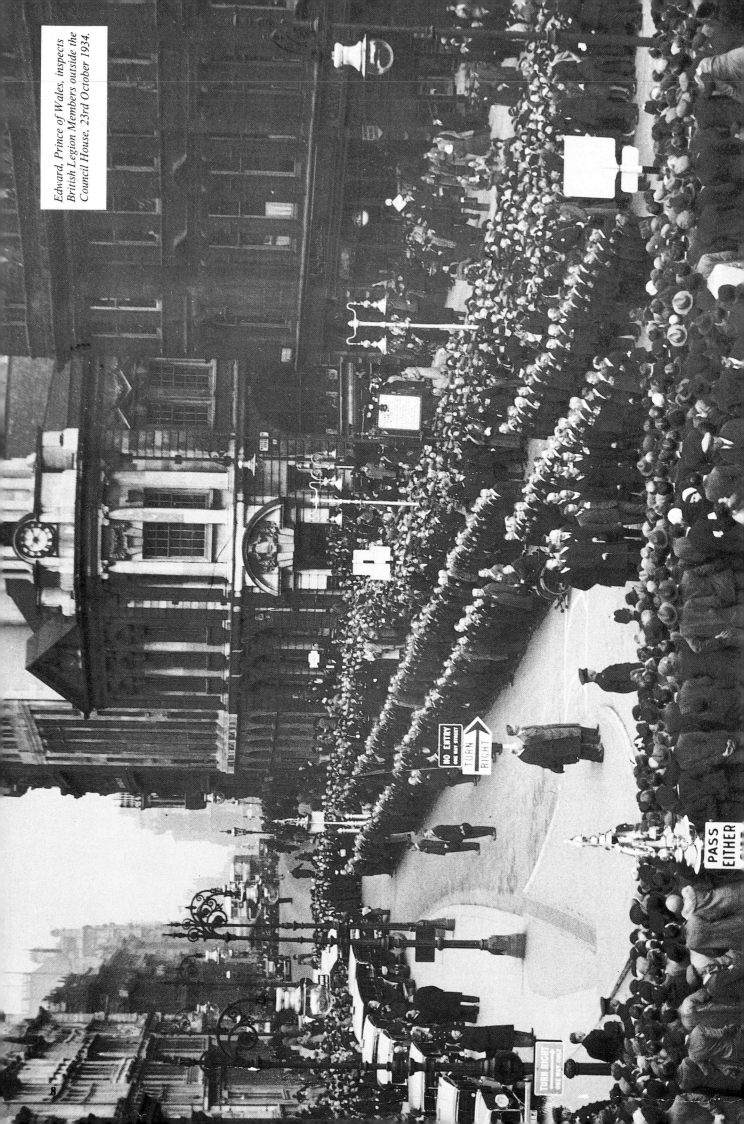

Edward, Prince of Wales, inspects British Legion Members outside the Council House, 23rd October 1934.

8

Evening Despatch

Newspaper House, Birmingham.

Telephone: Central 8461 (15 lines).
Telegrams: Evening Despatch, Birmingham.

THURSDAY, 10 DECEMBER, 1936

THE KING'S SACRIFICE

K ING EDWARD VIII. has, after days of anxious thought—anxiety shared by all sections of the British people throughout the Empire—decided to abdicate.

We are probably too near the event to realise the mighty significance that this surrender means; the crisis burst upon the country like a thunderstorm, and in what seems the turning of an hour an act fraught with vital concern to our Commonwealth has taken place.

The Birmingham Mail

TUESDAY, MAY 11, 1948

FORWARD IN LOYALTY

Birmingham is not a very demonstrative city, but in its solid British loyalty to the Crown it lives fully up to its motto. The welcome which it gives to the King and Queen to-day, however, is much more than merely loyal and dutiful: it is friendly and heartfelt in the full and time-honoured Midland measure. Birmingham's mind goes back to those wartime visits when their Majesties, with a minimum of fuss and no panoply, came to sympathise with us in our sufferings and to help us to face still undaunted and unflagging, the Herculean industrial effort that was our pride. Loyalty was infused with something of love and much of genuine admiration in that trying phase: Birmingham sensed true leadership of British stamp in a partnership of quiet mutual courage and happiness.

Industrially, Birmingham has long been one of the leading cities of the world and aimed to become one of the great hospital cities too. In 1920 the Hospitals Centre Scheme was originated. By 14th July 1938, the complex was ready to be opened by King George VI and his Queen, Elizabeth. Sadly, the King fell ill at that time and the Duke and Duchess of Gloucester deputised.
The Bishop of Birmingham offers a prayer of dedication. Among those present, the Lord Mayor, Coun. Ernest Canning, Neville Chamberlain (The Prime Minister) and Mrs Chamberlain.

The Lord Mayor and Lady Mayoress, Coun. and Mrs John Burman, walk with King George VI and Queen Elizabeth (now the Queen Mother) to the Council House, 11th May 1948.

9

The Duke of Edinburgh, with the Lord Mayor, Ald. Frank Price, arrives to open the Bull Ring Centre, 29th May 1964.

Princess Margaret arrives to open the Birmingham Post and Mail Buildings, 26th October 1965. With her is the Chairman, Sir Eric Clayson (right) and her then husband Anthony Armstrong-Jones (now Lord Snowdon).

After a performance of "First Impressions" Princess Margaret talks to Patricia Routledge and Francis Matthews. She had just officially opened the New Repertory Theatre, 20th Ocotber 1971. Also present was actor Sir Felix Aylmer, who spoke the very first words on stage at the Old Rep in 1913.

SEEMING at times almost lost in the width of her limousine, a dainty woman, whose pictures can do her less than justice, proved she is Queen of Hearts in the West Midlands.

Her title of Elizabeth II, by the grace of God, of the United Kingdom of Great Britain and Northern Ireland and of her other realms, Queen, Head of the Commonwealth, Defender of the Faith, has an awe-inspiring ring.

But West Midlanders welcomed her as a beloved leader due to become a grandmother in her Silver Jubilee Year — and simple affection was the keynote of her 13-hour visit to the heart of her kingdom.

She chose a heavy silk apple green coat and dress, its matching turban dotted with white flowers on its organza, to brighten the day the weathermen warned might turn to drizzle.

"Like your Mum only posher and she doesn't carry a shopping basket all the time."

That was young Miles Wilson's view of the Queen as he waited near the Hall of Memory

He is 12 and lives in Erdington.

This was a Birmingham city centre converted to carnival atmosphere with bands, with red, white and blue flowers, office workers in best clothes — even a bunch of Chelsea Pensioners got their own special cheer as they waited for the Royal procession.

Most of all, it was flower power. With dozens of children dashing to give the Queen posies as her walkabout took her through Chamberlain Square.

27/7/78

Princess Alexandra, Patron of the Junior Red Cross, talks to a squad of cadets at the opening of the ATV centre, Bridge Street, 10th May 1970. This is now known as Central TV.

Prince Charles is shown around Longbridge, 22nd October 1980.

The Queen Mother arrives to open the Queen Elizabeth II Law Courts, 18th November 1987. On the same day, she unveiled a plaque marking the centenary of the Foundation of the Victoria Law Courts.

BIRMINGHAM AT ARMS

"The small arms arsenal of the world" was a tag which came to be attached to Birmingham, and not without reason. The Birmingham Small Arms (BSA) Works in Armoury Road, Small Heath, produced rifles and ammunition at very short notice during the Boer War (1889-1902) and continued its vital work during the two World Wars which followed. In fact the First World War was described as "a struggle between Krupps (the German armaments giant) and Birmingham". In 1914 volunteers for the army were styled the 1st, 2nd and 3rd Birmingham Battalions, later to be incorporated into the Royal Warwickshire Regiment. They distinguished themselves on the Western Front in France. Birmingham pioneered food rationing so successfully in 1917 that the Government adopted the scheme nationally. Three times Zeppelins (German airships) reached Birmingham and one night in October 1917 several bombs were dropped on the Austin Works at Longbridge. There were no casualties.

The Second World War was a very different matter. Seventy-seven air-raids brought a death toll of 2,241 citizens with 6,692 injured. 140,336 homes were damaged, 12,125 badly. In addition 4,003 business premises, 2,365 factories and workshops suffered damage. The Market Hall was completely burnt out on 26th October 1940; the Empire Theatre was destroyed on 28th October 1940 and the Prince of Wales Theatre on 9th April 1941. The city's worst raid was on 19/20th November 1940 when 23 districts were hit with 646 heavy bombs, 18 parachute mines, 243 batches of incendiaries, 17 oil bombs and 48 unexploded bombs. The longest raid, lasting 13½ hours, occurred on 11th December 1940. However, Birmingham picked itself up, dusted itself down and prepared to withstand anything further the enemy could throw - and the city aquitted itself nobly, due in no small measure to the efforts of ordinary people - boys and girls, air-raid wardens, firemen, messengers, police, ambulance crews, nurses and so many others.

Your King & Country need you.

Will you answer your Country's Call? Each day is fraught with the gravest possibilities, and at this very moment the Empire is on the brink of the greatest war in the history of the world.

In this crisis your Country calls on all her young unmarried men to rally round the Flag and enlist in the ranks of her Army.

If every patriotic young men answers her call, England and her Empire will emerge stronger and more united than ever.

If you are unmarried and between 18 and 30 years old will you answer your Country's Call? and go to the nearest Recruiter—whose address you can get at any Post Office, and

Join the Army To-day! 5/8/14

The Birmingham Technical School, Suffolk Street, becomes the recruiting headquarters, 1914.

Recruiting Parade, Windmill Street, 1914.

Drum-Head Service, Victoria Square, 1916.

BSA workers take part in the "Win the War" celebrations in Cannon Hill Park, 21st September 1918.

PEOPLE CEASED WORK

When the maroons announced the signing of the Armistice with Germany on November 11, 1918, the whole country went wild with rejoicing. By general consent all work was suspended, shops were shut and schools were given holidays. Within a few hours Birmingham was bedecked with flags. Practically no work was done.

County Fire Office Limited,
Midland Branch,
59&61. Colmore Row.
Birmingham. 29th March 1919.

Miss Elsie S.Wanty has been in our employ for more than three years and is leaving us in consequence of the return of our Staff from the Army. During the time she has been with us she has always been attentive to her duties, proved herself to be reliable, capable and trustworthy in every way and I have pleasure in supporting any application she may make in connection with a clerical appointment.

District Manager.

BIRMINGHAM PARISH CHURCH
St. Martin's, Bull Ring.

UNVEILING OF THE
Birmingham City Battalions
𝔐emorial

14th, 15th and 16th BATTALIONS
THE ROYAL WARWICKSHIRE
REGIMENT

Sunday, 12th November, 1933
3.30 p.m.

Evacuees leave Snow Hill Station, September 1939.

AFS Station, Geraldine Road, Hay Mills, September 1939.

Protection for the Town Hall, August 1939.

All ready for the worst. Thousands of gas masks awaiting distribution in an Air Raid Precaution Store, September 1939.

John Bright Street, smashed and barely recognisable, 19/20th November 1940.

WE HAD IT WORST– AND DIDN'T FLINCH

PAYING tribute at a Birmingham luncheon yesterday, attended by the Duchess of Gloucester, to the way in which Birmingham had stood up to air raids, the Bishop of Fulham said: "It has won the admiration of the whole country."

The Lord Mayor, Councillor Wilfrid Martineau, said that although there were some scars on what the late Mr. Chamberlain had described as "the dear dirty old face" of Birmingham, her Highness could see for herself that the spirit of the people remained as unbroken as ever in their belief of victory.

It was disclosed yesterday that one of a series of four successive night raids on the city a few weeks ago was described as the fiercest experience by any town in the country since the raids began.

15. 11. 40

P.C. Ronald Jackson (right) was the first policeman in the city to be awarded the George Medal for gallantry during the blitz. Buckingham Palace, October 1941.

TUESDAY, MAY 8, 1945

"MADE IN BIRMINGHAM"

War Weapons Forged in the City

Victory Won in the Workshops

THERE is an old saying that the Battle of Waterloo was won on the playing fields of Eton. It might well be said that the European war which commenced in 1939 was won in the workshops of Birmingham.

Women's Auxiliary Police Corps, Bridge Street, 1944.

VE celebrations, Billesley, May 1945.

The Birmingham Mail

6·30

LIGHTING-UP TIME, 9.34 p.m.

Nº 24,785   WEDNESDAY, AUGUST 15, 1945   ONE PENNY

WORLD-WIDE REJOICING AT END OF WAR

ROYAL FAMILY ON PALACE BALCONY

JAPANESE CABINET RESIGNS: WAR MINISTER'S SUICIDE

SCENES OF WORLD-WIDE REJOICING TO-DAY MARKED THE END OF THE WAR WITH JAPAN. IN EVERY ALLIED COUNTRY PEOPLE WENT WILD WITH DELIGHT. LONDON WAS WELL TO THE FORE, FOR THE DAY COINCIDED WITH THE STATE OPENING OF PARLIAMENT, AND HUGE CROWDS GAVE THE KING AND QUEEN A RAPTUROUS RECEPTION. VICTORY BELLS PEALED FROM WESTMINSTER ABBEY AND ST. PAUL'S.

In his speech opening Parliament the King said: "The surrender of Japan has brought to an end six years of warfare which have caused untold loss and misery to the world," said the King in his speech to Parliament. "In this hour of deliverance it is fitting that we should give humble and solemn thanks to God, by Whose Grace we have been brought to final victory.

"My armed forces from every part of my Commonwealth and Empire have fought with steady courage and endurance. To them, as well as to all others who have borne their share in bringing about this great victory, and to all our Allies, our gratitude is due. We remember especially at this time those who have laid down their lives in the fight for freedom."

On their return from Westminster the King and Queen, with the two Princesses, appeared on the balcony of Buckingham Palace just before one o'clock, and were given a tremendous reception.

Their Majesties repeatedly waved to the thousands standing out in front of the Palace and the crowd waved back and sang "For He's a Jolly Good Fellow."

The aerial system of a transportable Radar station, as used for detecting enemy aircraft.

Emperor's Message to His People

WAR WOULD RESULT IN OBLITERATION

Speaking over the radio for the first time in the history of Japan, the Emperor told the people to-day of the acceptance of the Allied terms.

At the same time the Japanese News Agency, describing the scene when the decision was made, said: "All the Ministers and military and naval chiefs were profoundly impressed by the gracious concern of his Majesty for his subjects and the country, and silently bowed in obedience and wept."

"To our good and loyal subjects," Hirohito said: "After pondering deeply on the general trend of world and actual conditions obtaining in our empire to-day, we have decided to effect a settlement of the present situation by resorting to an extraordinary measure.

"We have ordered our Government to communicate to the Governments of the United States, Britain,

empire towards the emancipation of East Asia.

"The thought of those officers and men, as well as others who have fallen on the fields of battle, of those who died at their posts of duty, or those who met with (word not heard clearly but probably "untimely") death, and all their bereaved families, pains our heart night and day.

"The welfare of the wounded and war sufferers and of those who have lost their home and livelihood are objects of our profound solicitude. The hardships and sufferings to which our nation is to be subjected hereafter will certainly be great.

Dictate of Time and Fate

"We are keenly aware of the inmost feelings of all our subjects. However, it is according to the dictate of time and fate that we

LORD MAYOR'S CALL

"LET US THANK GOD FOR VICTORY"

In a message to the citizens of Birmingham, the Lord Mayor said that their first thought was one of gratitude that after practically six years of war peace had been proclaimed.

The end of the European War and the finish of the war in the Far East had been successfully accomplished, but not only by the skill and sacrifices of our fighting services or by the munitions of war. Like so many others, he was happy in his belief that Almighty God came to our aid.

The feeling of thankfulness was saddened by the knowledge that many homes could never be the same. Let them thank God for the bravery and self-sacrifice of those who died defending their comrades.

"Help the Maimed"

There were many who would return maimed in body or mind, and he was thinking of all who had near and dear ones in the Far East, maybe as prisoners of war. They looked to their swift and safe return, and to each other to help re-establish them

THE KING OPENS PARLIAMENT

"VICTORY EFFORTS" NEEDED TO HELP INDUSTRY

EXTENDED PUBLIC OWNERSHIP

Reconversion of industry from war to peace was given a foremost place in forthcoming domestic legislation outlined in the King's Speech to Parliament to-day.

It is intended also to secure "by suitable control or by an extension of public ownership that our industries and services shall make their maximum contribution to the national well-being."

For the solution of these difficult problems the King called on the people for "efforts comparable in intensity and public spirit to those which have brought us victory in war."

Planned Investment

Other outstanding points in the Speech included:—

Employment.—Machinery will be set up to provide for the planning of investment. The Bank of England and the coal mines will be brought under public ownership.

Housing.—Resources of the building and manufacturing industries will be organised to increase the number of homes available.

Demobilisation.—"Orderly release" of men and women on plans announced in the autumn will be continued.

Trade Unions.—The Trades Disputes and Trade Unions Act will be repealed.

URGENT TASKS OF RECONSTRUCTION

WAR SACRIFICES SHALL NOT BE IN VAIN

The King, in his speech, said: *My Lords and Members of the House of Commons.*

It is the firm purpose of my Government to work in the closest co-operation with the Governments of my Dominions and in concert with all peace-loving peoples to attain a world of freedom, peace and social justice, so that the sacrifice of the war shall not have been in vain.

To this end they are determined to promote throughout the world conditions under which all countries may face with confidence the urgent task of reconstruction and to carry out in this country those policies which have received the approval of my

port trade and of securing by suitable control or by an extension of public ownership that our industries and services shall make their maximum contribution to the national well-being. The orderly solution of these difficult problems will require, from all my people, efforts comparable in intensity and public spirit to those which have brought us victory in war.

In order to promote employment and national development, machinery will be set up to provide for the effective planning of investment, and a measure will be laid before you to bring the Bank of England under public ownership. A Bill will also be laid before you to nationalise the coalmining industry as part of a concerted plan for the co-ordination of the fuel and power industries.

Legislation will be submitted to you to ensure that during the period of transition from war to peace there are available such powers as are necessary to secure the right use of our commercial and industrial resources and the distribution and fair prices of essential supplies and services.

Building of New Homes

An urgent and vital task of my Ministers will be to increase, by all practicable means, the number of homes available both in town and country. Accordingly they will organise the resources of the building, housing and other essential building requirements of the nation.

They will also lay before you proposals to deal with the problems of compensation and betterment in relation to town and country planning, to improve the procedure for the acquisition of land for public purposes and otherwise to promote the best use of land in the national interest.

You will be asked to approve

GLITTERING SCENES

CROWN ON CRIMSON CUSHION

For over an hour before the King arrived every entrance and by-way to Parliament Square and Whitehall was packed.

VE-Day crowds were small in comparison with this great host of jubilant celebrators.

In the House of Lords the chatter of the House was hushed as the blazing lights went up.

All rose. Lord Jowitt, a tall figure in his black and gold robes as Lord Chancellor, entered and stood aside as, with members of their suite carrying their wands of office and walking backwards before them, the King and Queen entered.

Immediately in front of them walked the Earl of Cork and Orrery, carrying the Imperial Crown on a crimson cushion.

The great jewels of the Crown glittered in the light. It was the first time the Crown has been seen on a ceremonial occasion since before the war.

The King led the Queen into the Peers' chamber, holding her white-gloved hand in his. She was wearing turquoise blue, with a small-brimmed hat to match.

Firm, Vigorous Tones

The King and Queen bowed low to the peers. The peers bowed back and the King took his place on the Throne, with the Queen on his left.

The King began to read the speech in strong, vigorous tones, with no trace of hesitation.

With other M.P.s Mr. Churchill stood as the King, taking the Queen's hand again in his, led her down the crimson-covered steps.

In slow procession the King and Queen moved out of the Chamber to return to Buckingham Palace, where hundreds of thousands of subjects were waiting to cheer them.

Many had been waiting since long before dawn to see their Majesties and their Sovereign's escort.

UNIONISTS DECIDE ON ATTACK

NATIONALISING PLAN TO BE RESISTED

(From a Lobby Correspondent.)

The King's speech sets out a long programme that bristles with controversies.

Bringing the Bank of England under public ownership is one of them. The Unionist Opposition, which has already met and discussed its general line of attack during the

18

MADE AND SOLD IN BIRMINGHAM

Because of poor communications and the high cost of road carriage at that time, Birmingham's craftsmen of the mid-18th century had to make as much as possible out of as little as possible. How well they succeeded! Around the time when city status was conferred, Birmingham had 745 trades listed and by 1914 there were few commodities which the city could not supply.

Herbert Austin came to Birmingham in 1893 and took charge at the Wolseley Sheep-Shearing Company, where, in 1901, the design of his three-wheeled car was bought from him by the newly-formed Wolseley Motors Ltd. He installed his own motor car works in derelict printing premises at Longbridge in the same year and wrought a 20th-century miracle of engineering. A four-cylinder tourer was first out of the factory in 1906 to be followed, in 1923, by the famous Austin Seven. And its price? - just £165! Herbert Austin's hopes of "motorising the masses" were about to be fulfilled. The accessory firms, like GEC, Dunlop and Joseph Lucas Ltd., employed thousands on their assembly lines. Lucas began as an oil merchant in Carver Street in 1875 and, using mass production by semi-skilled and unskilled labour, satisfied the growing needs of the motor car industry. John Boyd Dunlop patented his pneumatic tyre in 1888, produced his first samples in Aston and moved to Fort Dunlop in 1917.

Jewellers resisted the change to assembly lines and continued to employ highly-skilled labour, sometimes with as few as twenty workers per company. The Jewellery Quarter is still within the "Hockley Square Mile" near St Paul's, the "Jewellers' Church". Some firms there now were in existence prior to Birmingham becoming a city.

George and Richard Cadbury took over their father's cocoa and chocolate factory in Bridge Street, off Broad Street, and in 1879 moved to a large factory that they built in Bournville. The result was the foundation of the Bournville Village Trust in 1900 with a "model village" for their own workers as well as for others.

The Martineau family has had a long history of working for the city. Robert, Thomas, Ernest, Wilfrid and Denis Martineau all served as Mayors or Lord Mayors at some stage between 1846 and 1987.

Birmingham is renowned for the scope and variety of its industrial and commercial activity. Citizens employed in our shops, banks, travel agencies, insurance companies, bakeries, breweries, factories, places of entertainment, in the fast-growing Chinese Quarter and in numerous other spheres keep the city humming along.

The button spinning and burnishing shop, Firmin and Sons, New Town Row, c. 1905. The firm has been in the city for over 100 years and, apart from making the buttons for many national uniforms, also makes helmets for the Household Cavalry and manufactures a vast variety of metal pressings and stampings.

Albert Parsons files the barrel of a shotgun at W. Powell and Sons (Gunmakers) Ltd., Carrs Lane, 1952. He was one of three brothers employed by the firm, which, being founded in 1802, is one of the oldest in the city.

Remploy Ltd., Garretts Green Lane, 14th June 1967. The firm started in Kings Norton and Yardley and then moved to its present site in 1952. Remploy is the biggest employer of disabled people in Britain.

Joseph Lucas Ltd., Great King Street, Hockley, 19th September 1955.

Fort Dunlop, Castle Bromwich, 1961.

Austin Motor Works, Longbridge, September 1978.

Ronald Cartland, brother of Barbara, canvasses support from the workers at the caravan building firm Eccles, 1935. He won Kings Norton that year. Mr Cartland had the sad distinction of being the first M.P. to be killed in the Second World War.

Singer Motors, Coventry Road, Small Heath, July 1958. Thirty years later this site has been completely cleared.

Tea out! 1958

FOR a man who can just about understand how a hinge works, I must say that I was hardly the best pupil for a lesson on how a new coin-in-the-slot machine produces a steaming hot cup of tea in 11 seconds.

Still, I followed it all the way—from coin in to tea out.

When the machines shown in the Birmingham trade exhibition I visited come on the market, you will be able to buy tea, coffee and even hot pies by putting a coin in the slot.

The organisers believe that they will also change the pattern of canteen life in the factories.

An outsize generator leaving the GEC works, Witton, 20th July 1971.

A Leyland trolleybus, the Old Square, March 1932. This is one of the second generation of trolleybuses and even looked like a contemporary bus, with its crome radiator. From 1904 the bulk of the city's transport needs were in the hands of the Corporation. In 1969 West Midlands Passenger Transport Executive took over and then, from 1986, West Midlands Travel have been in charge.

"The City of Birmingham" (Princess Coronation Class), designed by Sir William Stanier in 1937 and built in June 1939. It was withdrawn from service in 1964 and can still be seen at the Museum of Science and Industry, Newhall Street.

SO YOU think life is tougher today? Not compared to 1952.

Souvenir hunters stripped the last trams to run on Birmingham's Bristol and Pershore Road routes.

Housewives queued for days to get the sales bargain they wanted — boxed jackets of wool for 29s 11d and dresses at less than a pound.

But when the Queen came to Claerwen to open the dam that was to give us all the water we ever thought we might need — mourning for her father George VI over — we all looked for a brighter, more prosperous Sec Elizabethan Age.

Austerity was still with us — though this was the when the man whose name will be forever asso with it — Sir Stafford Cripps — died.

That meant rationing. Like meat: varying fr 2d-worth to 1s 5d worth — about half a pound of "c meat." Tea was increased from 2oz to 2½oz (at a lb) — though there were cheers when it was free rationing at the end of the year. You could have of bacon at 3s 5d lb. It was the year of pride in the — and the year of disaster in the air and on land. was king — and a killer.

The war in Korea dragged on — while peace talks Panmunjon seemed an endless stalemate.

Winston Churchill's Government battled for the sa ends as today — solvency and economy — and the Labo opposition was split by Aneurin Bevan and his followe pressuring Mr. Attlee.

1962

Television cameras at work at the Stock Exchange, 20th August 1958.

At work at the Trunk Test Desks, Telephone House, 8th January 1937.

Birmingham Exchange and Engineering Centre, Stephenson Place, 7th March 1954. The newly-opened centre was used as a meeting place for firms and for short-term exhibitions. There was office accommodation available and an extensive library.

Early work on the Birmingham Hospitals Centre, 9th October 1934. (Now the Queen Elizabeth Medical Centre).

Hamstead pit is closed

1965

THE PIT they said would outlive even the youngest of its miners brought the last shift to the surface in March.

Hamstead Colliery — the only mine within the Birmingham area — closed its gates, the machinery silenced — while underground lay 20,000,000 tons of coal that would never be brought to the surface.

The reason: geo-logical faults in the seams — some with shifts of as much as 50 feet — which made mechanical mining uneconomic if not impossible.

Since 1947 £2,000,000 had been spent on modernisation in efforts to make it pay.

And the gamble, estimated to have left the Coal Board with a £1,500,000 operating loss — apart from the capital expenditure and interest charges, had failed.

HP Sauce started life orginally as the Midland Vinegar Co. in Tower Road, Aston. The name "HP" was registered in 1896 and in 1903 the Houses of Parliament design came into being. In 1972 the company was renamed Smedley-HP Goods Ltd. An engrossing book "The Road from Aston X" told the story in detail in 1975.
Shown here is a 1969 product.

27

Ansells' Brewery, Aston Cross, c. 1959.

The College Arms, Stratford Road, Hall Green, 1st November 1935. Back to delivery methods from a byegone era - or a publicity stunt? Whatever, it makes a lovely picture.

Davenports Brewery Promotion, 1986.

BOURNVILLE
COCOA IS FOOD

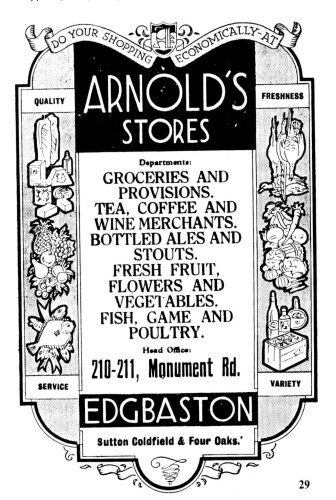

Helen Parker puts the finishing touches to some of her exhibits at a chocolate demonstration, 5th December 1956.

The first six milkmen and stablelads of the Birmingham Industrial Co-operative Society, Newdigate Street, 1920.

Cadbury's mobile cafe which supplied, as an advertising experiment, free samples of steaming cocoa to householders, January 1938. Interesting features of this vehicle included a gas cooker, a stove and a sink with running water. Music was supplied from gramophone records.

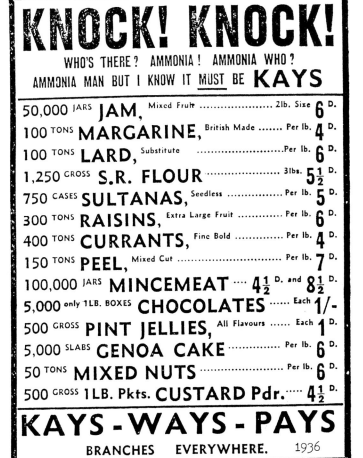

W. Pond & Co., exhibit at Bingley Hall, c. 1910. Their shop was in Steelhouse Lane, but now they trade in Corporation Street, opposite the

Municipal Bank, 163 Stratford Road, Sparkbrook, 15th August 1919.
Now part of the TSB Group.

Flora Wright and her daughter Nellie look into the sunshine from the
door of their shop in Bromsgrove Street, Summer 1928.

Post Office, Middlemore Road/West Heath Road, 1937.

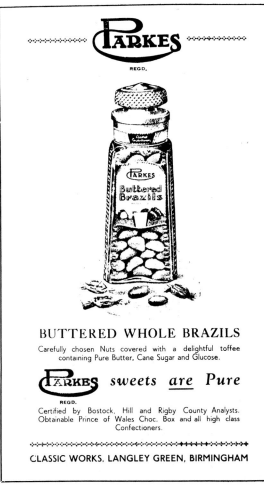

THE SMITHFIELD MARKET

In Moat Row stood the manor house of Peter de Berminghar dating from the 12th century and this remained, afte rebuilding, until the end of the 18th century. In 1881 th Smithfield Market was erected on the site, when its founda tions had to be sunk to 14 feet to get below the mud of th ancient moat. This market was extended in 1903 and th whole was demolished in stages in 1975, revealing remains c the old manor house. A new wholesale market nov flourishes, having been erected progressively on the forme market site.

1901.

1905.

Moat Lane, c. 1936.

1938.

SPORT

Association Football has always been popular in Birmingham as seen in the early and continued support of our two major clubs, Aston Villa and Birmingham City. The Villa were one of the famous twelve clubs which formed the basis of The Football League in 1888. In 1895 they won AND lost the F.A. Cup in the same season! It was displayed in a shop in New Town Row, from where it was stolen and never recovered. The famous "double" of League title and F.A. Cup (1897) has been followed by numerous competition successes. Appropriately, in the 1988/89 season, having clinched promotion, they are again amongst the elite in Division 1. Birmingham City (The Blues) were founder-members of Division II in 1892 and stepped up into Division I in 1894. The club's name at this time was Small Heath Alliance and changed to Birmingham in 1905; "City" was added in 1945. The Blues won the Football League Cup in 1963, ironically having to beat the Villa to do so! Our two major teams have brought fame to the city and long may they continue to do so.

To William Ansell, in 1882 the headmaster of Bristol Street South Board School, fell the task of co-ordinating the various types of cricket being played in Warwickshire and he became the first Secretary of the Warwickshire County Cricket Club, originally styled a "team" and not a "club". One of the finest grounds in England was opened at Edgbaston in 1886 and in 1902 a Test Match (England v. Australia) was allocated to Birmingham for the first time. The County Championship became Warwickshire's in 1911, 1951 and 1972. They won the Gillette Cup in 1966 and 1968 and the John Player League in 1980.

Nigel Mansell, from Hall Green, winner of over a dozen Formula One races, has new hope of fulfilling his ambition to win the Grand Prix motor-racing drivers' world championship as he joins the Ferrari team in his city's centenary year. He was runner-up in 1986 and 1987.

The Birmingham Anglers' Association was formed in 1883 and is now the largest angling association in the country, having 640 affiliated clubs and 25,000 members.

The West Midlands Region of the Sports Council, with offices in Metropolitan House, Hagley Road, was established by Royal Charter in 1972 to develop and improve the knowledge and practice of sport and physical recreation in the interest of social welfare and the enjoyment of leisure among the public at large. The staff are advisers with experience of sport and recreation.

Latch and Batchelors F.C., Hay Mills, winners of the Wire Masters Cup, 1939.

Birmingham City F.C. 1962-63
LEAGUE CUP WINNERS

Back row (from left): Mr. Gil Merrick (manager), G. Sissons, P. Wright, S. Lynn, L. Brown, J. Schofield, C. Withers, P. Bullock, Stubbs, B. Sharples, Ken Fish (trainer). Seated: M. Beard, M. Hellawell, J. Bloomfield, J. Harris, K. Leek, T. Hennessey, J. Sing W. Foster, J. Watts, M. Clarke, B. Auld. On ground: B. Farmer, J. Regan, G. Farrell, B.. Rushton, T. Wolstenholme, D. Thwait W. Atkinson, R. Martin. Inset: Trevor Smith.

—AND FOR YOUR AUTOGRAPH ALBUM . . .

Aston Villa fans acclaim their team's winning of the F.A. Cup, Villa Park, 1957.

Aston Villa players after their promotion to Division I, 7th May 1988.

The founder members of Selly Oak Old Boys R.F.C., 1963. The present team (now known as Selly Oak R.F.C.) became champions of the North Midlands Division 3 League in 1988, their Jubilee year.

Six rugby players from Moseley F.C., all of whom played for England. Standing (left to right) Nigel Horton and Sam Doble. Seated, Jan Webster, John Finlan, Colin McFadyean and Keith Fielding, 24th October 1972.

The battle for the British flyweight title between Birmingham's Bert Kirby and Manchester's Jackie Brown, fought at the old West Bromwich skating rink in 1929, still reigns as the last British championship to be contested on a Sunday.

●

It was October 13, unlucky for the Brummie who was K.O.d in the third. Five months later Kirby took sweet revenge when he went to London and put Brown down in the third to bring the championship to Birmingham.

Kings Heath Cricket and Football Club celebrated their hundred years in June 1968 and, as part of a week-long series of events, the Hockey Club First Eleven (seen here) played the Worcestershire County Team. As no football had been played there for many years, the club changed its name to Kings Heath Cricket & Sports Club and still has its ground and clubhouse in Alcester Road South.

Mouse had 'em roaring

1962

IT WAS ON May 31 that a classic bat and mouse game had them roaring on the stands and rolling with laughter in the pavilion.

It happened as England skipper Ted Dexter was at the crease in the first Test against Pakistan at Edgbaston.

Dexter took his stance, faced the bowler-then something caught his eye that distracted him.

Sitting close to the crease was, of all things, a mouse ... small, brown and totally bewildered.

He waved his arm and the bowler skidded to a halt. The crowd roared as Dexter looked down at the mouse ... and the mouse stared back.

It was some time before it ran off. But throughout lunch it remained sitting in the playing area.

Official record books apart, the little mouse stepped into history that day and reports of the match carried the line: "Mouse stopped play." Dexter went on to make 72 and England won by an innings and 24 runs.

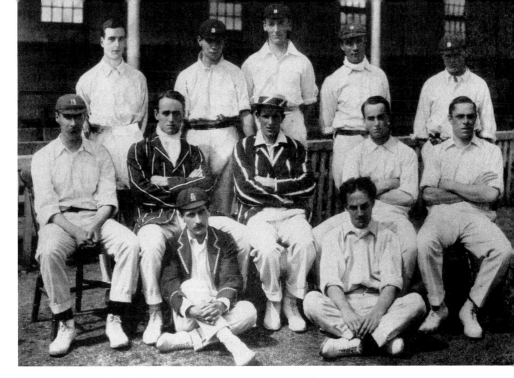

Warwickshire C.C.C., County Champions, 1911.

Warwickshire C.C.C., County Champions, 1951.

Warwickshire win the Gillette Trophy by beating Worcestershire at Lords, 3rd September 1966.

Birmingham-born Dennis Amiss triumphantly registers his 100th century, in the match against Lancashire at Edgbaston, 29th July 1986.

37

Celebrity cricket match, Edgbaston Ladies' C.C. v Birmingham Women's C.C. (The latter was formed in 1928 and is the oldest club in the city). 12th July 1982.

The city's own Ann Haydon-Jones shows the Ladies' Plate, won at Wimbledon, to the Lord Mayor and Lady Mayoress, Ald. and Mrs Neville Bosworth, 10th July 1969. Her husband Pip Jones proudly looks on.

Ray Barber and Grace Smith, winners of The Birmingham Post Golfer of the Year titles at Kings Norton, receive their trophies from N.J. Reedy, Editor of the Post, 27th April 1975.

Small Heath Harriers gather on the steps of their HQ, the Bulls Head, Hay Mills, in 1934. The club celebrates its centenary in 1991.

The opening day of the summer season at Northfield Swimming Baths, 13th April 1958.

The Handsworth Wood Bowling Club Ltd., Devonshire Road, the oldest level green club in the city, celebrate their 75th anniversary, 13th August 1968. On this occasion they made it a "Good Old Days" event.

Beacon Road-Cycling Club's 21st Anniversary Dinner at the Black Horse, Northfield, 1967.

39

The start of the Formula 3000 Race in the first Super Prix, Bristol Street, 25th August 1986.

ENTERTAINING THE CITY

Moving pictures first came to the Birmingham area in 1888 when Pat Collins, the showman, gave screenings in Aston. By 1938 the city had over 90 cinemas, most with twice-weekly changes of programme in addition to a separate Sunday showing. We all had our favourite local "flea-pit" but something altogether special was that trip to the city centre - perhaps to the Odeon, New Street; the Gaumont, Steelhouse Lane; the Forum, New Street; or the Scala, Smallbrook Street. The stylish Beaufort, Coleshill Road, Washwood Heath, was an outstanding suburban cinema from its opening in 1929 to its demise in 1978.

Perhaps the live theatre was a parallel attraction for us. The Theatre Royal, New Street, was built in 1774 and suffered disastrous fires in its lifetime but, after being rebuilt in 1904, it survived until final closure on 15th December 1956. The Woolworth Building was erected on the site. The Aston Hippodrome remained a theatre from 1908 until 1960, when bingo took over, and demolition followed in 1980. The Birmingham Hippodrome, Hurst Street, failed to attract the public when first opened in 1899 as the "Tower of Varieties and Circus". Refurbished, it became the "Tivoli Theatre" in 1900 and the Hippodrome in 1903. There were more building changes in 1919 and 1979 (when the freehold was purchased by the City of Birmingham) and in 1984 with a new, vast stage and the comfort of air-conditioning. Its seating capacity is now 1,943. We have mentioned Sir Barry Jackson's Repertory Theatre elsewhere in this book. Its replacement, in Broad Street, was opened on 20th October 1971, having seats for 901, its adjacent auditorium, The Studio, seating 120. The Alexandra Theatre, John Bright Street, first opened its doors on 27th May 1901 as the "Lyceum", gaining its present name a year later. It was acquired by the Birmingham Corporation in 1969. Leon Salberg, who died in 1937 and his son, Derek, who retired in 1977, directed the theatre with distinction.

The new City of Birmingham Show is an annual three-day event in Perry Park where the best flowers, honey, cage-birds, rabbits, dogs, horses, etc. are on view.

Edgbaston Reservoir, of some 78 acres, provides recreation for large numbers of anglers and for boaters. Close by is the Tower Ballroom, a popular venue for all kinds of dancing.

The Birmingham Ice-Rink in Pershore Street has its counterpart for roller-skaters at the Handsworth Leisure Centre, Holly Road, which also caters for badminton, basketball, netball, volleyball and swimming.

The Midland Arts Centre, Cannon Hill Park, is operated by the Cannon Hill Trust, which was established in 1962. It has its own Puppet Theatre and Music Theatre set in 15 acres of beautiful surroundings and it invites visiting theatre and dance groups to entertain patrons.

The Botanical Gardens at Westbourne Road, Edgbaston, have 15 acres forming an oasis of tranquillity just one mile from the city centre. They are open every day of the year except Christmas Day. The Hugh Nettlefold Garden of alpines, rock gardens and pools, was established in 1893.

The City of Birmingham Symphony Orchestra, since its formation as the City of Birmingham Orchestra on 5th December 1920, has emerged as an orchestra of immense, worldwide stature and, with its TV and radio broadcasts, records, tapes and regular foreign tours, it is taking Birmingham's name to every corner of the globe. Its popular conductor, Simon Rattle, follows in a long line of famous conductors such as Sir Adrian Boult, Leslie Heward, George Weldon, Rudolph Schwarz, Hugo Rignold and Louis Fremaux.

A sheer delight is an event called "Aston Hall by Candlelight" staged in the Hall in late autumn. No modern lighting is used, yet the Long Gallery, the fine contemporary staircase and elaborate plaster ceilings are seen in a magical setting.

A newer annual event is the Birmingham International Jazz Festival, which started, in a small way, in 1984. Conceived and organised by Jim Simpson, it now attracts musicians, singers and audiences from all over the U.K., and even beyond.

Theatre Royal, New Street, prior to its closing in 1902.
After rebuilding it was open again on 16th December 1904.

21st birthday celebrations at the Repertory Theatre,
Station Street, 1934. Sir Barry Jackson (second left) greets
members of the company.

Aston Hippodrome, 1935.

Grand Theatre, Corporation Street, July 1937. It eventually became The Grand Casino Ballroom and closed in 1960.

PRINCE OF WALES THEATRE

BIRMINGHAM

Commencing MONDAY, MAY 1st. FOR TWO WEEKS !

Every Evening at 7.30

MATINEES (Reduced Prices) : THURSDAY AND SATURDAY at 2.30

'Phone: MIDLAND 5684 (3 Lines). Box Office Open 10 a.m. to 9 p.m.

FIRTH SHEPHARD

PRESENTS

THE ACTUAL COMPANY and PRODUCTION FROM THE GAIETY THEATRE, LONDON

RUNNING RIOT

THE FUNNIEST MUSICAL SHOW OF THE YEAR

By DOUGLAS FURBER

From a Plot by GUY BOLTON and FIRTH SHEPHARD

Music and Lyrics by VIVIAN ELLIS

Dances and Ensembles arranged by JACK DONOHUE   Costumes designed by RENÉ HUBERT

Produced by LESLIE HENSON & HERBERT BRYAN

LOUISE BROWNE
ROY ROYSTON

MARY LAWSON   GAVIN GORDON

DEBROY SOMERS AND HIS BAND

JOHN E. COYLE   ROSALIND ATKINSON

RICHARD HEARNE
FRED EMNEY

LESLIE HENSON

" MADE EVERYONE ACHE WITH LAUGHTER."
— EVENING STANDARD.

HATPINS

SIR,—During the pantomime at a Birmingham theatre last Christmas my husband had a very unpleasant experience which might have had very serious consequences.

A lady behind him had pinned her hat to the seat, and as he stood up to allow someone to pass the hatpin ran into his back and broke.

He did not like to make a scene so came home, and I drew from his back a length of hatpin quite three inches long.

M. T.

December 16, 1910.

PROGRAMME

"Birmingham Weekly Post."

TWENTY-SEVENTH ANNUAL

UNCLE JOHN'S POOR CHILDREN'S

Christmas Party

TOWN HALL

(Kindly granted by the Lord Mayor, Alderman W. W. Saunders)

FRIDAY, JANUARY 16th, 1931

43

BRITAIN'S one and only Prime Minister of Mirth, Sir George Robey, knighted at the New Year — died in November, aged 85.

The man whose songs like "Another Little Drop" and "If You Were the Only Girl in the World" had been among the best-loved, longest-lived favourites for millions of people round the world.

He made his first appearance in Pershore Road, Birmingham, in the little church hall with corrugated iron roof at St. Mary and Ambrose.

Genius

Although born in Kennington and christened George Edward Wade, the comic genius had his first job in a Birmingham civil engineer's office and George went on to a job as a clerk of works on the city's first cable tramway from Colmore Row to Hockley.

When he turned professional he called himself "Roby" from the name of a Birmingham firm for whom he worked, and later, when it tended to become mis-spelt he accepted it as "Robey."

Playing Dame in "Robinson Crusoe" for Derek Salberg at the Alexandra Theatre in 1938, he fell off the stage and broke three ribs.

Remembered as a red-nosed comic in a bowler and collarless coat with a cane to whirl, Sir George had ranged from panto and music-hall through musical comedy, light opera to Falstaff.

1954

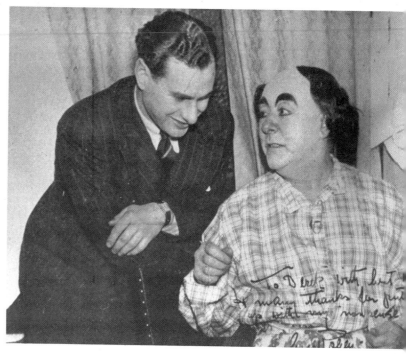

Derek Salberg, Managing Director of the Alexandra Theatre, chats with George Robey, 16th February 1939. Mr Salberg is now a successful writer with several books to his credit.

The old entrance to the Alexandra Theatre, John Bright Street, 2nd June 1938.

44

HIPPODROME
BIRMINGHAM

Proprietors: MOSS' EMPIRES, Ltd.
Chairman: PRINCE LITTLER   Managing Director: VAL PARNELL   Telephone: MIDLAND 2576/7
Manager and Licensee: BERTIE ADAMS

6.15 ★ Week Commencing MONDAY, JULY 30th ★ **8.30**
TWICE NIGHTLY

MAKING HER FIRST VARIETY TOUR OF GREAT BRITAIN

THE BEAUTIFUL
YANA
Television's Exciting Singing Personality
At the Piano: TOMMY WOLF

MORECAMBE & WISE
RADIO AND TV's POPULAR COMEDY STARS

EDDIE GORDON & NANCY	GRANGER BROS	FREDDIE HARRISON	ELEANOR GUNTER & PARTNER
THE SILENT HUMOURIST	DYNAMIC DANCERS	TRICKY PIANIST	CONTORTIONS IN BALANCE
	CHERRY WAINER		
	BRITAIN'S BRILLIANT RHYTHMIC ORGANIST		

Roy Rogers

Johnnie Ray

Richard Burton

1954 WAS the year when Trigger, Roy Rogers' near-human horse trod the carpets of the Queen's Hotel, Birmingham — after an hysterical reception from a crowd of 5,000.

Led from the luxury horse-box in which he had travelled from Edinburgh, Trigger bowed to a cheering throng which was held back by nearly 100 police.

With his own teeth he signed the visitors book at the hotel before trotting up the stairs to Room 170 for a brush down.

But he spent the night in a stable secretly set aside in Holiday Street.

Roy, Trigger and Dale Evans (Mrs. Rogers) were at the Hippodrome for the week — a show in which Roy did a little sharp-shooting, sang a song or two, asked his young audience to clean their teeth and go to Sunday School, while Trigger danced and did some simple sums.

NORMAN WISDOM — came back in a variety show at the same theatre — and the crowds jammed Hurst, Street with hundreds of people without tickets, prepared to wait and cheer him away.

BIRMINGHAM was packed with fans of another kind on the following

Sunday when the singing idol, crooner Johnny "Cry" Ray had to be smuggled in and out of the Hippodrome.

"This is one of the wildest audiences I have ever faced," said Johnny — the only disappointment being that he produced no tears.

IN OCTOBER it was the turn of Frankie Lane — apart from the crowds at the theatre he was marooned in the Queen's Hotel after one abortive attempt to go out of the swing doors.

In five seconds the nearest of the 500 fans had robbed him of a handkerchief and all the buttons off his dress jacket.

Lady Barnett — TV star, house planner, magistrate, mother and deputy mayoress came back to Birmingham to open an exhibition — as the darling of "What's My Line?"

It was her first since the previous August when her appearance in a Town Forum panel from the Central Fire Station, led to What's My Line? and made her a national figure.

A NEW screen revolution came with the advent of Cinemascope — the giant "letter box" picture that promised almost stereoscopic reality.

It came with "The Robe" at the Odeon, New Street, the Biblical epic which put actor Richard Burton — an unknown figure to Hollywood until he won this part — on the road to fame.

Norman Wisdom

Lady Isobel Barnett

Thirty four years later Frankie Laine was back at the Hippodrome, 1st May 1988, to a full house and a tumultuous reception.

Tony Hancock, born in Hall Green, back in the city to top a variety bill, rehearses with the Betty Fox Dancing Teenagers, 2nd September 1957.

Sparkbook's Sid Field appears with Margaret Lockwood in the film "Cardboard Cavalier", 1949.

The Scala Cinema, Smallbrook Street, 2nd December 1953. It closed in 1960, when the Ring Road was being constructed, and a second Scala opened 4 years later (now known as the Odeon, Queensway).

Bristol Cinema, Bristol Road, December 1955. It was demolished in 1988.

Curzon Hall, Suffolk Street, was reconstructed in the mid-twenties and became the West End Cinema. It closed ten years after this picture was taken. 9th July 1957.

The Plaza, Stockland Green opens, Boxing Day 1927. It closed 45 years later.

Victoria Picture House, Green Lane, Small Heath, July 1951. It closed six years later. Most regulars referred to it as the "Green Lane Cinema".

The Birchfield Picture House, Birchfield Road, Perry Barr, 11th August 1952, served the area from 1913 for almost half a century.

48

The Odeon, Birmingham New Road/Hagley Road West, July 1953. In 1961 it became a bowling alley.

The Tyseley Cinema, Warwick Road, Greet, July 1954. It closed in November 1959 with a showing of "Six Bridges to Cross".

The Era Picture Playhouse, Bordesley Green, surely the quaintest of all the city's cinemas, January 1958, just thirteen months before its closure.

★ YOUR ENTERTAINMENT GUIDE ★

THEATRES

ALEXANDRA THEATRE
Friday 7.15. Saturday 5 & 8.
VIVIEN LEIGH, CLAIRE BLOOM
"DUEL OF ANGELS"
With FREDA JACKSON: ROBIN BAILEY.
21st (for 2 weeks): Derek Salberg's Repertory Company in "DISTINGUISHED GATHERING."
Box Office 10—7.15. MID 1231.

REPERTORY THEATRE
18th MARCH — 19th APRIL
"THE TEAHOUSE OF THE AUGUST MOON" by John Patrick. Evenings 7.0. Matinees, Wednesdays and Saturdays 2.30. Usual agents. Now Booking "Dagger's Point" and Type B Season Tickets. Box Office (MIDland 2471) open 10.0 a.m.—7.30 p.m.

SHAKESPEARE Memorial Theatre
1958 SHAKESPEARE SEASON
Until April 19th: "Romeo and Juliet." Book now! Civic Radio Service, 27b Paradise Street (MID 0021). Evgs. 7.30. Mats. Thurs., Sat. 2.30.

BIRMINGHAM HIPPODROME
Twice Nightly, 6.15 & 8.30.
Welcome Return of "Fabulous"
CHARLIE GRACIE
Brilliant Young Singing Star of "Disc Jockey Jamboree."
April 21st: MICHAEL HOLLIDAY; HAL MONTY & His Company.
Box Office 10—9. MID 2576/7. Agencies

BIRMINGHAM HIPPODROME
Matinee Sat., April 26 Comm. 2 p.m.
JOAN HIPKISS
presents her School of Dancing in
HUMPTY DUMPTY
Tickets on sale Hippodrome Box Office and Lewis's from Monday, April 21. Prices 5/-, 3/6, 2/6 and 1/6. 5/- and 3/6 reduced for children.
The past five Annual Theatre Shows at the Plaza Theatre, West Bromwich, completely sold out.
Book early and avoid disappointment
Proceeds to Ebenezer Church, Old Meeting Street and Swan Village Methodist Church.

ASTON HIPPODROME
6.20—8.30 Phone AST 2341
OASTON and ANDREE Present
"STRIP SCANDALS"
with Dave Gray, the Sensational Melfi Kids, Toni Kaye, Joan and Paul Sharrat, etc.
Behind the Scenes in London after dark.
Old Age Pensioners 1/- Monday and Tuesday 6.20. B.O. 10—7.

WINDSOR THEATRE
BEARWOOD
Mon.-Fri. 7.30. Sat. 6.15 & 8.30.
Famous Players in
"RANDOM HARVEST"
Enthralling Play by
MOIE CHARLES & BARBARA TOY.
21st: "BREAKFAST IN BED."
Box Office 10—8. BEA 2244. Free Park.

CRESCENT THEATRE
BIRMINGHAM 1. April 26th—May 10th, at 7 p.m.: "THE CRUCIBLE" (Arthur Miller). Theatre box office opens Saturday, April 19th, from 2-4 p.m., thereafter from 6-8 p.m. each weekday until the play ends. From Monday, April 21st., seats may be reserved at Civic Radio Services, Paradise Street (who will also accept new members), from 10 a.m. to 5 p.m. daily. Members only.

COVENTRY

THE COVENTRY THEATRE
Friday 7.30. Saturday 2.30 & 7.30
THE ROYAL BALLET
(Formerly Sadler's Wells Theatre Ballet). Repertory includes 3 NEW BALLETS. April 21: "SAILOR BEWARE," with TESSIE O'SHEA. 28th: COVENTRY FESTIVAL OF MUSIC — Famous Orchestras, Conductors, Soloists. May 5: "YOU TOO CAN HAVE A BODY" (BILL MAYNARD, BILL KERR). May 12: DICKIE VALENTINE. B.O. 10—8. COV 3141.

WEDNESBURY

WEDNESBURY HIPPODROME
This Week
H. J. Barlow presents the GALLEON THEATRE COMPANY in the comedy
"EASY MONEY"
Nightly 7.30. Fri. 8.0. Sat. 6.0 & 8.15
Box Office (WED 0634) open 10—8
Licensed Bars. Free Car Park

ICE SHOW

EMBASSY SPORTSDROME
WALFORD ROAD, BIRMINGHAM
"WINTER WONDERLAND"
ICE SPECTACULAR OF THE AGE
NOW EXTENDED ONE EXTRA WEEK
UNTIL APRIL 26th
Book LEWIS'S TRAVEL BUREAU
And at Embassy Sportsdrome
12/6, 10/6, 7/6, 5/-, 3/6
Nightly 7.30 p.m. Matinees Wednesday 3 p.m.; Saturday 2.0, 5.0, 8.0 p.m.
Half price children all performances (except Sat. 8 p.m.).
Reduced prices for parties of 20 or more any day.
Hundreds of additional seats now available at 5/-, 3/6.
Seats at door at all prices for all performances.

CINEMAS

TATLER THEATRE
STATION STREET
Continuous Daily 10.15.
Prices 1/3 and 2/1.
IT'S CARTOON AND COMEDY TIME
TOM AND JERRY
GARDEN OF EATIN
ONE NOTE TONY
TWEETIE—STOOGES—SYLVESTER

CINEMAS

ODEON NEW STREET — MID. 6101 — Cont 10 a.m.
Laurence HARVEY, Dawn ADDAMS, John CLEMENTS, Michael CRAIG,
"THE SILENT ENEMY" (U)
The story of Cmdr. Crabb
at 10.50 a.m., 2.5, 5.20 and 8.35.
"WELCOME YOUR MAJESTY" (U) In Eastman Colour—H.M. The Queen Mother's tour of Australia. At 10 a.m., 1.10, 4.20 and 7.35 p.m.

CINEPHONE — MID 1761 — Bristol Street
She has an astonishing figure and displays most of it . . . Press.
MARISSA ALLASIO as
GIRL IN A BIKINI (U)
(Italian with English sub-titles)
at 2.15, 5.35, 9.5. Also
WERNER PETERS in
DER UNTERTAN (A)
(The Underdog). (sub-titles)
An Outstanding German Production at 12.40, 4.0, 7.30.
Coffee Lounge open 10.30—11.30 p.m.

GAUMONT
Steelhouse Lane. CEN 3014.
Continuous 12.0. Last Comp. Prog. 7.0.
18 TOP RECORDING STARS . . .
15 RHYTHM HITS in the
BEHIND THE RECORD STORY OF
THE BIG BEAT (U)
Eastman Colour.
Screened at 2.0, 5.35, 9.05.
HEDY LAMARR : GEORGE NADER
JANE POWELL : JAN STERLING
THE FEMALE ANIMAL (A)
Screened at 12.20, 3.50, 7.20.

WEST END
Retained for further week
ALEC GUINNESS in
THE BRIDGE ON THE RIVER KWAI (u)
Technicolor
Today at 1.25, 4.30, 7.40
To the many new friends we made during 'Around the World' we would strongly recommend this film, which is quite OUTSTANDING

ABC FORUM — Today Cont. 10.05. — MID 4519
RETAINED SECOND WEEK
JOHN MILLS
RICHARD ATTENBOROUGH
BERNARD LEE
DUNKIRK (U)
Showing at 10.55, 2.0, 5.05 and 8.10
Eric Barker : Thora Hird
CLEAN SWEEP (U)
Showing at 10.05, 1.05, 4.15 and 7.20.

A.B.C. BRISTOL — Cont. 1.30 — Bristol Rd. — CAL 1904
ALAN LADD
THE DEEP SIX (U)
(WarnerColor)
Dianne Foster, William Bendix, Keenan Wynn
Presented at 2.35, 5.35, 8.35
Lyle Bettger,
EXPLOSION (A)
1.35 4.40 7.40

FUTURIST — Theatre MID 0292 — Cafe MID 1579
Retained 3rd Week
Ernest Hemingway's
"A FAREWELL TO ARMS" (A)
Technicolor
starring
ROCK HUDSON
JENNIFER JONES — VITTORIO DE SICA
Screened at 1.35, 4.40, 8.15
Doors open 12.45. Last perf. 7.15
*Admission prices for this Exclusive Presentation, in advance of its Autumn Release, are STALLS 3/6, 5/-. CIRCLE 6/6, 7/6
A 20th Century-Fox
CINEMASCOPE PICTURE

SCALA — Theatre MID 0578 — Free Car Park
Presents
Retained Second Week
TERRY-THOMAS
JOYCE GRENFELL
GEORGE COLE
in
"BLUE MURDER AT ST. TRINIAN'S" (u)
Guest Star: ALASTAIR SIM
Also SABRINA
At 2.50, 5.45, 8.46
JIM DAVIS ARLEEN WHELAN
in
"RAIDERS OF OLD CALIFORNIA" (u)
At 1.20, 4.18, 7.15. L.P. 7.15

NEWS THEATRE
MID 0260. HIGH STREET
Daily from 10.30. 1/3 and 2/1 only
STOP, LOOK, LAUGH
LARRY SEMON
3 3 3
CARTOONS
PANAMA PLAYGROUND. Travel
WORLD NEWS. INTEREST.

Let's go to the Pictures — CINEMATOGRAPH EXHIBITORS' ASSOCIATION — *Denotes 6-day Programme

ABC ADELPHI, Hay Mills. VIC 1208. HAPPY IS THE BRIDE (u) 2.25, 5.40, 8.50; THE TALL TROUBLE (u). Sun: Five Against the House (a).

ALBION, New Inns, HANDSWORTH. Pat Boone, Shirley Jones, APRIL LOVE (u) Eastman Col.; Audrey Trotter, GHOST DIVER (u).

ABC ALHAMBRA, Moseley Road. VIC 2826. Ian Carmichael, HAPPY IS THE BRIDE (u) 2.25, 5.40, 8.55; THE TALL TROUBLE (u).

APOLLO, Tyburn Road — ERD 0834. THE GYPSY AND THE GENTLEMAN (a) Col; Rock Pretty Baby (u). L.P. 7.0. Sun: Betrayed (u).

ATLAS, Stechford — STE 2206. Jane Powell, GIRL MOST LIKELY (u); TENNESSEE'S PARTNER (a) Col. Sunday: Sitting Bull (u).

BEACON — GREAT BARR. Pat Boone, APRIL LOVE (u); C Scope, Eastman Col.; Wild Bill Elliott, BITTER CREEK (u).

BEAUFORT — WASHWOOD HEATH. Pat Boone, Shirley Jones, APRIL LOVE (u) C Scope, Eastman Col.; James Craig, GHOST DIVER (u).

BIRCHFIELD, Perry Barr. BIR 4333. Richard Widmark, TIME LIMIT (a); Anne Heywood, THE DEPRAVED (a). Sun. 3.30: Law v Billy the Kid (u).

CAPITOL — WARD END. Michel Ray, THE BRAVE ONE (u) Tech; ROMMEL'S TREASURE (u), Col. Sunday: Tumbleweed (u).

CARLTON, Sparkbrook — SOU 0861. Cameron Mitchell, ESCAPADE IN JAPAN (u); Day of the Badman (a) C Scope. Sun: The Raiders (u).

CASTLE CINEMA — CAS 2425. Gene Kelly, LES GIRLS (a) 2.45, 5.35, 8.25; The Story of Ruth (u). Sun: Son of Ali Baba (u).

CLIFTON — GREAT BARR. Disc Jockey Jamboree (u) (Sat. 2.30) 5.30; The Green Eyed Blonde (a). Sun: Mississippi Gambler (u).

CORONET, Small Heath — VIC 0420. Michel Ray, THE BRAVE ONE (u) C/S Tech; ROMMEL'S TREASURE (u) C Scope Tech.

CROWN, Ladywood (ABC) EDG 1122. Pat Boone, Shirley Jones, APRIL LOVE (u) C/Scope Col; James Craig, Ghost Diver (u) R/Scope.

ABC EDGBASTON — EDG 3273. DISC JOCKEY JAMBOREE (u); THE GREEN EYED BLONDE (a). L.P. 7.0. Sun: Green Fire (u) Col.

EITE, Handsworth — NOR 0665. Jerry Lewis, THE SAD SACK (u) V/Vis., Rhonda Fleming, Those Redheads From Seattle (u) Tech.

EMPRESS, Sutton (ABC) SUT 2363. Pat Boone, Shirley Jones, APRIL LOVE (u) Col; James Craig, GHOST DIVER (u) L.P. 7.0.

ERA CINEMA BORDESLEY GREEN. Norman Wisdom, JUST MY LUCK (u); John Saxon, SUMMER LOVE (u). Sun: Against All Flags (u).

ESSOLDO, Longbridge — PRI 2470. APRIL LOVE (u) 2.0, 5.25, 8.55; PLUNDER ROAD (u). L.P. 7.5. Sunday: Command (u).

ESSOLDO, Quinton — WOO 2562. Pat Boone, APRIL LOVE (u); PLUNDER ROAD (u). L.P. 7.15. Sun: The Human Jungle (a).

GAIETY, Coleshill St. (ABC). CEN 0649. Robert Mitchum, Curt Jurgens THE ENEMY BELOW (u) C/Scope, Col.; THE FLYING SCOTT (u).

GAUMONT, SMETHWICK. SME 0950. CHICAGO CONFIDENTIAL (a); THE IRON SHERIFF (u). L.P. 7.20. Sunday: The Brave One (u).

GRAND, Alum Rock Road. EAS 0471. THE GIRL MOST LIKELY (u); DANGEROUS MOONLIGHT (u). Sun: Red Skies of Montana (a).

GRANGE, Small Heath — VIC 0434. Richard Burton, BITTER VICTORY (a); Decision at Sundown (u). Sun: Escape From Fort Bravo (a).

GROVE CINEMA, Dudley Road. SME 0343. Pat Boone, Shirley Jones, APRIL LOVE (u) C/Scope, Eastman Col., 2.10, 5.30, 8.40.

IMPERIAL, Moseley Rd. (ABC). CAL 2283. Pat Boone, Shirley Jones, APRIL LOVE (u) C/Scope, Col.; James Craig, GHOST DIVER (u).

KNIG'S NORTON — KIN 1079. MEN IN WAR (a) 2.0, 5.20, 8.40; Not Wanted on Voyage (u). LP 7.5. Sunday: Meet Me at the Fair (u).

KINGSTON, Small Heath — VIC 2639. Pat Boone, Shirley Jones, APRIL LOVE (u); James Craig, GHOST DIVER (u).

KINGSWAY — HIG 1352. Pat Boone, APRIL LOVE (u) 2.5, 5.20, 8.40; ROCK A BILLY BABY (u) 3.44, 7.5. L.P. 7.5.

LUXOR — CAL 2008. Alan Ladd, Clifton Webb, BOY ON A DOLPHIN (u) C/Scope, Col. Sunday: Horizons West (a) Tech.

LYRIC — PARADE. Burt Lancaster, The Kentuckian (u), C/Scope, Col; Lost Lagoon (u). Sun: Valley of the Kings (u).

MAJESTIC — BEARWOOD. Peter Finch, Windom's Way (u), Col; Th., Fri. 5.35, 8.35, Sat. 2.35, 5.35, 8.35; The Big Chance (u).

MAYFAIR — PERRY COMMON. DANGEROUS EXILE (a); Appointment With a Shadow (a). L.P. 7.8. Sun: Lawless Breed (a).

MAYPOLE, King's Heath—MAY 2051. The Tarnished Angels (a), C/Scope 5.30, 8.47; Damn Citizen (a). L.P. 7.7. Sun: Strange Lady in Town, u

MOSELEY PICTURE HOUSE.— Martin & Lewis, SCARED STIFF (u); Stranger at My Door (u). Sunday: Human Jungle (a).

NEWTOWN PALACE — ASTON. REVOLT AT FORT LARAMIE (u); THE LOST LAGOON (u). Sun: Bullet Is Waiting (u), Tech.

NORTHFIELD CINEMA — PRI 1463. Kirk Douglas, PATHS OF GLORY (a); Baby Face Nelson (a). L.P. 7.35. Sun: Johnny Guitar (a).

OAK, Selly Oak (ABC) — SEL 0139. Pat Boone, APRIL LOVE (u), Col; Ride a Violent Mile (u). L.P. 7.0. Sun: Wings of the Hawk (u).

ODEON, Blackheath — BLA 1036. RUN OF THE ARROW (u), Tech, 3.30, 8.15, 9.5; Professor Tim (u), 2.20, 5.5, 7.50. L.P. 7.45.

ODEON — KINGSTANDING. The Gypsy and the Gentleman (a), 1.25, 5.10, 9.0; An Eye for an Eye (a), 3.15, 7.0. L.P. 7.0.

ODEON — PERRY BARR. BITTER VICTORY (a); DECISION AT SUNDOWN (u), Tech. Sun: Robert Mitchum, Gung Ho (a).

ODEON — SHIRLEY. Richard Burton, BITTER VICTORY (a), C.S. 2.40, 5.50, 9.0; Decision at Sundown (u), 4.10, 7.20.

ODEON — SUTTON. Richard Burton, BITTER VICTORY (a), 2.26, 5.40, 8.55; Decision at Sundown (u), 4.0, 7.15. L.P. 7.15.

ODEON, WARLEY — BEA 1549. BITTER VICTORY (a), 2.35, 5.45, 9.0; Decision at Sundown (u), 4.5, 7.20. Sun: Too Late for Tears (a).

OLTON CINEMA — ACO 0593. Michel Ray, THE BRAVE ONE (u); ROMMEL'S TREASURE (u). L.P. 7.0. Sun: Rogue Cop (a).

OLYMPIA, Ladypool Road—VIC 0124. John Calvert, DARK VENTURE (u), Col; The Tomahawk Trail (u). Sun: The Great Game (u).

ABC ORIENT, Aston — NOR 1645. DISC JOCKEY JAMBOREE (u); THE GREEN EYED BLONDE (a). L.P. 7.10. Sun: Green Fire (u).

PALACE, Erdington (ABC) ERD 1623. APRIL LOVE (u) 1.45, 5.15, 8.45; GHOST DIVER (u) 3.25, 6.55. Sun.: Devil's Canyon (a).

PALLADIUM, Hockley (ABC)—NOR 0380. APRIL LOVE (u), Tech, 2.0, 5.25, 8.55; GHOST DIVER (u). Sun.: The Desert Legion (u) Tech.

A.B.C. PAVILION, Stirchley. KIN. 1211. Disc Jockey Jamboree (u). 2.25, 5.40, 9.00; The Green Eyed Blonde (a). LP 7.10. Sun.: Special Delivery (u).

ABC PAVILION, Wylde Green. ERD 0224. Disc Jockey Jamboree (u); The Green Eyed Blonde (u); L.P. 7.10. Sun.: Tight Spot (a).

PICCADILLY, Sparkbrook. (A.B.C.). VIC.1688. APRIL LOVE (u) C/S col.; RIDE A VIOLENT MILE (u); R Scope. L.P. 6.50.

PICTURE HOUSE, Aston Cross. (ABC). EAS. 0430. Rod Steiger Run of the Arrow (u) R Scope Tech; Professor Time (u). Sun: Big House USA (a)

PLAZA, Stockland Green. ERD. 1048. Michel Ray THE BRAVE ONE (u); 2.00, 5.20, 8.55; Dawn Addams Rommel's Treasure (u); 3.40, 7.10.

PRINCES, Smethwick. — SME. 0221. I Was a Teenage Werewolf (x); Dragstrip Girl (a). Adults only. Sun: Don't Go Near The Water (u)

A.B.C. REGAL, Handsworth. NOR. 1801. Anna Neagle The Man Who Wouldn't Talk (u); The Crooked Circle (u). L.P. 7.10.

RIALTO, Hall Green. — SPR. 1270. Michel Ray THE BRAVE ONE (u); C/Scope Tech.; Dawn Addams ROMMEL'S TREASURE (u).

ABC RITZ, Bordesley Green. VIC 1070. Janette Scott, HAPPY IS THE BRIDE (u); Dale Robertson, THE TALL TROUBLE (u).

ABC ROBIN HOOD — Hall Green. THE MAN WHO WOULDN'T TALK (u); The Crooked Circle (u). Sun: The Beast from 20,000 Fathoms (x)

ROCK CINEMA — ALUM ROCK. Pat Boone, APRIL LOVE (u), C S. Tech; James Craig, GHOST DIVER (u) Regal Scope. L.P. 7.0

ABC ROYALTY, Harborne. HAR 1619. THE MAN WHO WOULDN'T TALK (u); The Crooked Circle (u). Sun: The Brave and the Beautiful (a).

RUBERY CINEMA — Rubery 193. THE BRASS LEGEND (a) 6.20, 9.5; LADY OF VENGEANCE (a). LP 7.40. Sun: City That Never Sleeps (a).

SHELDON CINEMA — SHE 2158. Pat Boone, APRIL LOVE (u), C S Col.; GHOST DIVER (u). L.P. 7.15. Sunday: The Beachcomber (a).

SOLIHULL — SOL 0398. Jerry Lewis, THE SAD SACK (u) V/Vis.; CONQUEST OF SPACE (u).

SPRINGFIELD — Stratford Road. Peter Finch, THE SHIRALEE (u); IT'S A DOG'S LIFE (u), C Scope. Sunday: Valley of Kings (u).

STAR CINEMA — EAS 0461. Doris Day, THE PAJAMA GAME (u); HAND OF FATE (u). Sunday: Witness to Murder (a).

TIVOLI — COVENTRY ROAD. Michel Ray, THE BRAVE ONE (u); ROMMEL'S TREASURE (u). Sun: The Man From the Alamo (u)

TRIANGLE, Gooch Street—CAL 1060. Tommy Trinder, You Lucky People (u); Man on the Road (u). Sun: Ambush at Tomahawk Gap (a).

ABC TUDOR, King's Heath—HIG 1161. Abbott & Costello, Jack & The Beanstalk (u), 1.50, 5.30, 9.5; Alan Ladd, Drum Beat (u), 3.15, 6.50.

TYSELEY, Warwick Road—ACO 0133. BEST THINGS IN LIFE ARE FREE (u), C/Scope; APACHE WARRIOR (u). Sunday: Apache (u).

VICTORIA — EAS 0179. Witness for the Prosecution (u); Gun Duel in Durango (u). Sun: The Lawless Breed (a).

VILLA CROSS — NOR 0807. THE BRAVE ONE (u), C/Scope, Tech, 2.0, 5.25, 8.50; Rommel's Treasure (u), 3.35, 7.0. L.P. 7.0.

WALDORF — SPARKBROOK. Gary Cooper, Dorothy Maguire, FRIENDLY PERSUASION (u)), C/S Col. Sun: Golden Ivory (u).

WARWICK — ACOCKS GREEN. Harry Secombe, Ron Randell, DAVY (u), Tech; The Hired Gun (u). Sun: Horizons West (a).

WEOLEY, Weoley Castle—HAR 1490. Kirk Douglas, PATHS OF GLORY (a). BABY FACE NELSON (a). L.P. 7.35

WINSON GREEN — NOR 1790. Paul Newman, BOTH ENDS OF THE CANDLE (a), C/Scope. Sun: The Long Long Trailer (u).

WEST BROMWICH CINEMAS

IMPERIAL — WES 0192. The Brass Legend (a); Lady of Vengeance (a), plus Carmen Basilio v Sugar Ray Robinson Fight (u).

KING'S — WEST BROMWICH. John Wayne, Legend of the Lost (a) Tech. 2.0, 5.20, 8.40; Son of a Stranger (a) 3.35, 7.15.

QUEEN'S, West Bromwich—WES 0351. Runaway Daughters (x) Death Over My Shoulder (a). Adults only. Sun: Gorilla At Large (a) Col.

REX CINEMA — WED 0182. Dirk Bogarde, Ill Met by Moonlight (u), V/Vis; There's Always a Thursday (a). Sun: The Eternal Sea (u)

STONE CROSS — STO 2141. Jack Lemmon, OPERATION MAD-BALL (u) 2.22, 5.31, 8.49, Fri 5.31, 8.49; DOMINO KID (u). L.P. 7.15.

ABC TOWER — WES 1210. DISC JOCKEY JAMBOREE (u); The Green Eyed Blonde (a). Sun: It Came From Beneath The Sea (a)

DUDLEY PORT CINEMA

ALHAMBRA, Dudley Port — TIP 1400. Richard Widmark, Felicia Farr, THE LAST WAGON (u), C/S Col.; AT THE STROKE OF NINE (a).

GREAT BRIDGE CINEMA

PALACE, Great Bridge — TIP 1595. Margaret O'Brien, Walter Brennan, GLORY (u); No Time For Flowers (u). Sun: Eagles of the Fleet (u).

LANGLEY GREEN CINEMA

REGENT, Langley Green—BRO 1120. Elvis Presley, LOVING YOU (u); ESCAPE IN THE SUN (a). Sun: Where the River Bends (u).

WEDNESBURY CINEMAS

PALACE — WEDNESBURY. THE BIG CAPER (a); BUCKSKIN LADY (a). Sun: Tony Curtis, Beach Head (a).

RIALTO — WED 1686. J. Mansfield, Oh for a Man (u); In Times Like These (u). Sun: Down Among the Sheltering Palms (a).

DANCING

WEST END BALLROOM
Suffolk Street.
OPEN FOR PUBLIC DANCING
Monday Wednesday Friday.
Saturday, to
SONNY ROSE & HIS ORCHESTRA
Closed Tuesday and Thursday for private functions.
No admission after 10 p.m

TOWER BALLROOM
RESERVOIR RD., EDGBASTON
DANCING
Tuesday, Thursday, 8.0 3/-
Saturday, 7.30, 5/-

BOCKER, F.I.D.M.A., & BETTERIDGE, F.I.D.M.A.
65, BRISTOL STREET
MID 1022
CLASSES NIGHTLY (including Sun.) Tonight: Absolute Beginners 8.0-10.30 3/-. Tomorrow: 7.30 Inst. Complete Beginners. Practice Class 8.0-10.30 p.m. Entirely Private Lessons daily. 11.30-10.30
Start Now : Improve Your Dancing

ADELPHI BALLROOM
WEST BROMWICH
WES 1457
DANCING EVERY SATURDAY
7.30—11.30 p.m. Admission 4/-
SUNDAY CLUB (Members & Guests) Join Now. 7.30—11 p.m.
Sunday, April 27. Personal appearance of the British (and Star) Professional Ballroom Dancing Champions:
SONNY BINNICK and SALLY BROCK

CHATEAU IMPNEY
DINNER DANCE EVERY SATURDAY.
8 p.m.—12.0 21/- inclusive.
Evening Dress preferred.
Restaurant Open to Non-Dancers
Orchestral Teas every Sunday.
4—6 p.m. 6/6 inclusive.
For table reservations phone Droitwich 2362.

JOAN MILLER SCHOOL OF BALLROOM DANCING
ST. CHADS HALL,
Shireland Road, Smethwick
Tonight and every Friday,
Over 25 Class — 8 till 10. 2/-
Special Notice ! Friday, May 9
MEDAL PRESENTATION DANCE
BLUE GATES HOTEL,
High Street, Smethwick—7 till 12.
Licence 11. Demonstration by BOB AND JOAN AWFORD of Wolverhampton.
Compere Charles Capel 6-piece Orchestra
TICKETS 5/6

FRANK DOCKER'S DANCE SELECT
at MOSELEY BALLROOM
572 MOSELEY ROAD
(near Bus Depot)
Every Saturday Evening
7.30 p.m.—11 p.m., 5/-.

OPERA

Announcing the presentation of
GILBERT & SULLIVAN'S
"THE GONDOLIERS"
(by permission of Bridget D'Oyly Carte)
in the
MIDLAND INSTITUTE LARGE THEATRE
MAY 8th, 9th & 10th, at 7.0 p.m.
by the
BIRMINGHAM CO-OPERATIVE OPERA COMPANY
Admission Charges:
3/- (Centre Stalls); 2/- (Front & Back Stalls); 1/- (Side Stalls)
All seats reserved.
Tickets from the Birmingham Co-operative Education Department, High Street, Birmingham, 4, or obtainable at the Midland Institute on the evenings of the performances.

CONCERTS

TOWN HALL
TOMORROW
at 7.15 p.m.
YOUR FAVOURITE
OPERA AND BALLET PROGRAMME
featuring
THE FAMOUS OPERATIC SOPRANO
JACQUELINE DELMAN
with
ALFRED HALLETT
(TENOR)
AND THE FULL
ALBERT WEBB CONCERT ORCHESTRA
OF 40 PLAYERS
Tickets: 9/-, 7/6, 6/6, 5/6, 4/6, 3/-
from
CIVIC RADIO SERVICES,
PARADISE STREET, BIRMINGHAM
MID 1728/9.

SKATING

ICE SKATING RINK
CEN 6036-37
SUMMERHILL RD., BIRMINGHAM, 1
11 a.m., 2.30 p.m., 7.30 p.m. daily
It's Your Skating Season again.
Boots and Skates can be hired.

DANCING

THE BEST DANCES
WOOTTON HALL BALLROOM
WOOTTON WAWEN
Phone: Henley-in-Arden 323
Ballroom Dancing
EVERY SATURDAY
8—11.45 p.m. Admission 5/-
NO JIVING
AND THE BEST
FOUR HOURS
OF THE WEEK
BOOK OR COME EARLY AND AVOID DISAPPOINTMENT
(18)

A GALA NIGHT
with
JOE LOSS AND HIS ORCHESTRA
at the
ADELPHI BALLROOM
WEST BROMWICH
on FRIDAY, 25th APRIL, 1958
when
LAURA DIXON
will present under the auspices of the
SUNDAY MERCURY
THE MIDLANDS AMATEUR AND PROFESSIONAL CLOSED DANCING CHAMPIONSHIPS
also
FORMATION TEAM DANCING CONTEST
Dancing 8—1 a.m. Admission 7/6
Tickets available from the Sunday Mercury, Corporation Street; Branch Office, 166 High Street, West Bromwich, the Adelphi Ballroom, Laura Dixon Studios.

DANCE AT HAWLEY'S BALLROOM IMPERIAL
DUDLEY ROAD (near City Road).
A Welcome to All Members and Guests. Friday: "8.5 Special," (teenagers). Saturday: Ivan Langton and His Music. April 26: Talent Competition. Sunday: "Styx" Wilkinson Quintet.
"EVERY NIGHT AT EIGHT."

ROCK 'N' ROLL
EVERY SATURDAY
8.0 — 11.15 2/6
Over Burlington Restaurant next door Aston Hippodrome
Bus 33, 8 Inner Circle to Door (18)

TOWN HALL ORGAN

The Town Hall organ built in 1834 by William Hill was the property of the General Hospital until 1922. Various alterations and improvements to the organ were carried out in 1836, 1843, 1876 and 1890. In 1932 Henry Willis & Sons Ltd. were entrusted with the task of rebuilding the whole organ.

In 1950 the organ was cleaned without any of the works being dismantled and by 1963 a large scale cleaning was found to be necessary. This work, which was carried out between April and October 1964, involved dismantling 5,225 pipes in the organ, vacuuming inside and out, returning and installing humidifying apparatus. Since that date the "great" soundboard has been rebuilt.

The organ was completely rebuilt by N. P. Mander Ltd., during 1983-84 and was reopened on 6th October 1984 in time for the 150th Anniversary of the Town Hall. The console is on a different level and there are five manuals. The decoration of the front pipes has been restored by Anna Plowden Associates.

Lunch time concerts are organised by the city organist, Thomas Trotter, on most Wednesdays.

Simon Rattle, Principal Conductor of the CBSO, conducts the Birmingham Schools Orchestra at Lordswood Boys' School, Bearwood, 6th October 1984.

Jean Johnson's prize winning Olde-Tyme Junior Formation Team, 1962.

Sonny Rose, although not born in the city, was very much a part of its history. He was resident, on and off, from 1936 to 1959 at the West End Ballroom and then, by the strangest coincidence, became the musical director for the Holiday Inn, which stands on the site of the old West End.

The opening of the BBC Studios in Broad Street, 20th January 1926.

Harry Oakes and Gwen Berryman (Dan and Doris Archer of the long-running serial "The Archers") record their contribution to an everyday story of countryfolk for the BBC Midland Region, November 1955.

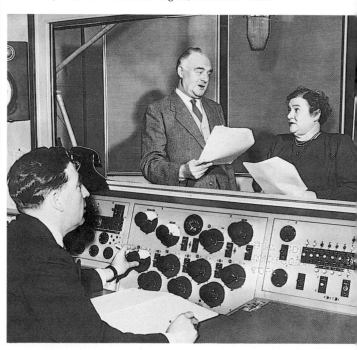

The Lord Mayor, Cllr. Marjorie Brown, signs in to officially launch BRMB Radio, 19th February 1974.

Birmingham's adopted son Ed Doolan, who moved to the city in January 1974 and within a month was on the air for BRMB. In September 1982 he moved to the BBC's Radio WM. Here, in 1983, (with a little help) he celebrates Australia winning the America's Cup.

Popular BRMB presenter Les Ross (born in Kingstanding) is interviewed by two hard-drinking guests, 28th August 1978.

Malcom Stent and Rosie, in the heyday of Radio WM's fictional "Barmaid's Arms", 1985. Malcolm was born in Saltley and Rosie in Aston.

Jasper Carrott, 1988, originally from Acocks Green, has become one of the country's top comics.

Barbara Cartland, in 1971, the world's most prolific authoress, was born at Vectis Lodge, Edgbaston, in 1901.

Temporary studio in use in Carpenter Road, September 1955.
The Gosta Green Studio opened four months later.

James Pestridge, Outside Broadcasts producer, in the
information room at Newton Street police station, 9th
September 1954. It was part of a series called "Ask a
Policeman", to be broadcast on the Home Service.

Sir Hugh Greene, Director General of the BBC, cuts the first
turf on the new site for the BBC Midland Region
Headquarters, Pebble Mill Road, Edgbaston, 7th April 1967.

The Lord Mayor, Ald. Garnet Boughton, cuts the tape to open
the Alpha Television Headquarters of ATV, Aston, 14th
December 1960. This took place after a major rebuilding
scheme, following several years of combined use by ABC TV
and ATV.

Northfield-born Ian Lavender, star of the TV programme
"Dad's Army", 1974.

Comedy pop group the Rockin' Berries present a cheque, on behalf of Goldliner Pools Ltd., to the Accident Hospital, much to the delight of young Patrick Walsh, 19th August 1981.

The cast of ATV's "Crossroads", c. 1969. The series began on 2nd November 1964 and ended 4th April 1988.

55

Rhoda Rogers Revuebar, Soho Road/Holliday Road, Handsworth, about to open, 12th August 19[..]

Bingley Hall, just prior to demolition in 1984.

EVENTS

Even by excluding happenings in Birmingham prior to 1889, and concentrating on highlights since that date, we would still need an elastic-sided book to record them all, so reluctantly we deal here with just a few special events - and "special" means anything from the birth of a child to a Grand Opening.

Joseph Chamberlain, a dynamic mayor between 1873 and 1876, when he resigned to take up a parliamentary career, left his mark on the city and indeed, his son, Neville, Lord Mayor himself from 1915 to 1917, also followed a career in politics and was Prime Minister from 1937 to 1939.

In the period 1904-1905, the Bishopric and Diocese of Birmingham was created.

During his time as Lord Mayor, Neville Chamberlain took up the option of creating the country's first and only Municipal Bank in 1916, setting up its head office in the basement of the City's Water Department. A stylish new head office opened in Broad Street in November 1933.

Birmingham's stature as a manufacturing city led quite naturally to the holding of the first British Industries Fair (B.I.F.) in 1925 at Castle Bromwich.

A progressive move was made in 1946 when the all-night bus service started and a year later the first City of Birmingham Show was staged in Handsworth Park.

The last tram journey on 4th July 1953 prompts us to note that in 1930 Birmingham Corporation had 843 trams, the largest fleet in the world.

Those who remember the old, noisy, smoky, steamy New Street station will also recall the new station being opened in 1967 to coincide with the electrification of the Birmingham to Euston line.

The £2 million Aston New Town Shopping Centre opened for business in 1968, practically opposite to the old Aston Hippodrome, which was demolished in 1980.

The Inner Ring Road, opened officially by the Queen in 1971, is aptly named Queensway. Two years later the Gravelly Hill Interchange (known as Spaghetti Junction because of its eight levels of intertwined road links) was opened and was the world's largest motorway intersection.

Symbolising Birmingham's place in the arts, a new concert hall, The Adrian Boult Hall, named after the famous conductor of the City of Birmingham Symphony Orchestra, was first used in December 1985. It had a seating capacity of 529.

In 1989 the Birmingham Mail Christmas Tree Fund celebrates 100 years of caring for the city's needy. In its time, the Fund has provided Christmas dinners, wireless licences, suits, blankets, coal vouchers, hot water bottles, knee rugs, tea, socks, boots and shoes. In recent years cash grants have been made. A small fleet of buses is the next aim. Altogether nearly £1½ million has been raised, and the target for centenary year is £100,000 which contrasts tellingly with the first year's donations in 1889 of £2. 11s. 4d. (£2.57p).

Perhaps the city's biggest enterprise of all is now under way - the International Convention Centre, providing conference and concert halls, hotels, restaurants, shops, banks and information points, all this on an extensive site near the demolished Bingley Hall between Broad Street and Cambridge Street. Completion is due in 1991 and will take Birmingham, the Big Heart of England, boldly into the 21st century.

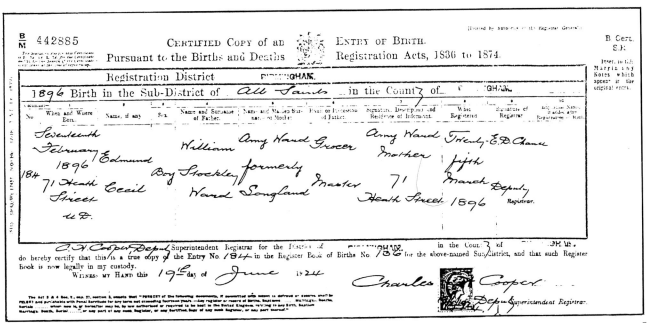

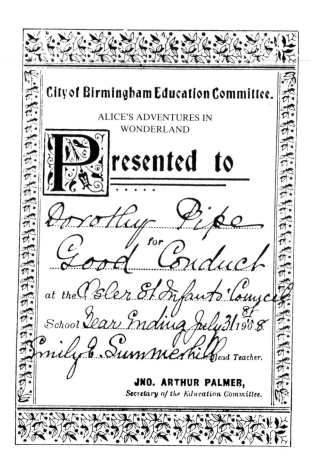

It was not until 1896 that Sir James Smith was raised from plain Mayor to become Birmingham's first Lord Mayor.

A day to remember in High Street, Harborne, Coronation Day (King George V and Queen Mary), 22nd June 1911.

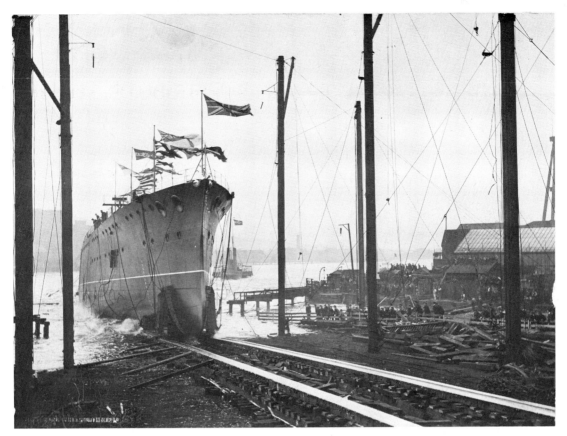

The light cruiser HMS Birmingham slides gently down the slipway at Armstrong Whitworth's yard on the Tyne, 7th May 1913. On 9th August 1914 she rammed and sank U15 off Fair Island (the first time a British ship had sunk a submarine). After a distinguished career she arrived at Pembroke Dock on 12th March 1931 to be broken up. The second HMS Birmingham was a 9,100 ton Southampton class cruiser built at Devonport Dockyard and launched on 1st September 1936. She served throughout the Second World War and supervised the surrender of the German Navy at Copenhagen in May 1945. She was broken up in 1960. The third HMS Birmingham is a Type 42 guided missile destroyer built by Cammell Laird at Birkenhead and launched on 30th July 1973.

The 100,000th Austin Seven comes off the production line, Longbridge, 1929.

The Central Fire Station under construction, December 1934.

The twenty-first anniversary of the 2nd Birmingham Boys' Brigade Company, Stratford Road Baptist Church, Sparkbrook, October 1934.

Jubilee Day in Heather Road, Small Heath, May 1935.

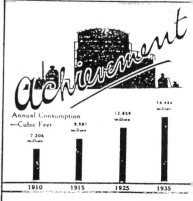

Let us look upon this momentous *Silver Jubilee of 1935* as a fit time for jubilation, a time for rejoicing that we, as a nation, have come so successfully through the troublous times of the World War; we can allow ourselves a feeling of triumph over the grave industrial crises since the war, and—on 6 May—surely none of us are too adult to allow ourselves a literal shout for joy that our beloved King and Queen are still at the head of a faithful and united Britain.

Long May They Reign

Jubilee party in Stour Street, Ladywood, May 1935.

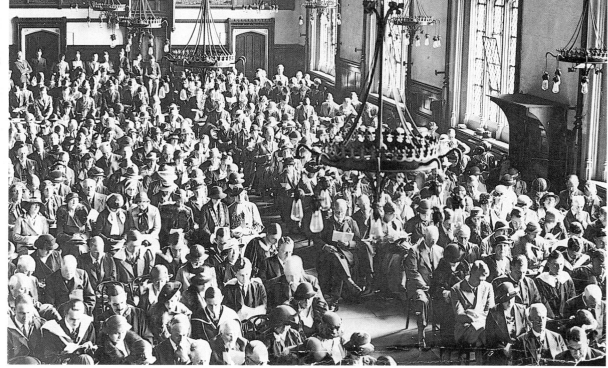

Speech Day, King Edward's School, New Street, 1st October 1935.

University Students Carnival, 1936.

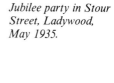

The cul-de-sac residents of Croydon Road, Erdington, in fancy Coronation style (George VI and Queen Elizabeth), May 1937.

The centenary of Joseph Chamberlain's birth is marked by the placing of a wreath at his statue, Chamberlain Square, 8th July 1936.

Smile, please! The children of Monica Road, Small Heath, face the cameras, Coronation Day, 1937.

A rehearsal for the Pageant at Edgbaston High School, 13th June 1938.

To mark the centenary of the grant of the Municipal Charter to Birmingham, celebrations on a grand scale were held in Aston Park from 11th to 16th July 1938. Local archers reinact the Battle of Crecy (August 1346). A fair proportion of the men-at-arms, in the actual battle, were born within the sound of St Martin's bells.

Honorary Freedom, City of Birmingham

Honorary Freemen and date when Honorary Freedom conferred

Joseph Chamberlain, M.P., 20th March, 1888.
Philip Henry Muntz, J.P., 23rd October, 1888.
Thomas Avery, J.P., 4th October, 1892.
George Dixon, M.P., 4th January, 1898.
John Thackray Bunce, J.P., 7th March, 1899.
Field Marshal Earl Roberts, V.C., K.G., O.M., 1st January, 1901.
Edward Lawley Parker, J.P., 31st October, 1904.
Jesse Collings, M.P., 13th June, 1911.
William Kenrick, J.P., 13th June, 1911.
Francis Corder Clayton, J.P., 2nd July, 1912.
Charles Gabriel Beale, J.P., 2nd July, 1912.
Sir William Bowater, J.P., 4th January, 1916.
W. M. Hughes (Australia), 22nd May, 1916.
David Lloyd George, O.M., M.P., 5th February, 1921.
Earl Balfour, K.G., O.M., 22nd June, 1922.
Sir George Hamilton Kenrick, 25th September, 1923.
Sir David Brooks, G.B.E., J.P., 25th September, 1923.
Sir Austen Chamberlain, K.G., P.C., M.P., 22nd February, 1926.
Barrow Cadbury, J.P., 6th May, 1932.
Neville Chamberlain, P.C., M.P., 6th May, 1932.
John Henry Lloyd, M.A., J.P., 6th May, 1932.
Ernest Martineau, C.M.G., D.L., 11th July, 1938.
William Adlington Cadbury, 11th July, 1938.
Wilfred Byng Kenrick, 11th July, 1938.
Henry James Sayer, J.P., 11th July, 1938.
Field-Marshal J. C. Smuts, C.H., K.C., 19th May, 1944.
Winston Leonard Spencer Churchill, C.H., F.R.S., M.P., 31st October, 1946.
Royal Warwickshire Regt., 1946, re-issued to Royal Regt. of Fusiliers, 7th May, 1975.
Clement Richard Attlee, C.H., M.P., 18th October, 1947.
General Sir William Slim, K.C.B., 18th October, 1947.
Sir Frank Henry Cufaude Wiltshire, M.C., 18th October, 1947.
Harrison Barrow, 12th April, 1949.
Mrs. Anne Marie Howes, M.B.E., J.P., 16th April, 1955.
Sir Barry Vincent Jackson, Kt., Hon. M.A. (Bir.), Hon. LL.D. (St. Andrews), Hon. D.Litt. (Bir.), Hon. D.Litt. (Manchester), 16th April, 1955.
Sir Sydney Vernon, LL.B. (Lond.), LL.M. (Birm.), 16th April, 1955.
Alderman Sir Theodore Pritchett, M.C., D.L., 7th May, 1960.
Alderman Sir Albert Bradbeer, J.P., 7th May, 1960.
268, Warwickshire Regt. R.A., T.A., 4th June, 1966.
Alderman F. F. Griffin and Alderman H. Watton, C.B.E., J.P. Hon. D.Sc., 2nd May, 1970.
35th (South Midland) Signal Regt. (Volunteers) R.Sigs., 12th September, 1970.
Alderman E. W. Horton, J.P. and Alderman E. E. Mole, O.B.E., J.P., 15th September, 1973.
H.M.S. "Birmingham," 11th May, 1978.
N. B. A. Bosworth, C.B.E., Sir Adrian Cadbury, M.A., Hon.D.Sc., J. Silverman, M.P., 4th December, 1982.
The Queen's Own Hussars, 17th May, 1985.
Mrs. Marjorie Alice Brown, C.B.E., J.P., 25th October, 1986.
Coun. Mrs. Freda Mary Cocks, O.B.E., J.P., 25th October, 1986.

The Freedom of the City is conferred upon (front row, from left to right) Sir Frank Wiltshire, General Sir William Slim and the Prime Minister, Clement Atlee, the Town Hall, 18th October 1947.

The Rt. Hon. Anthony Eden takes the salute from the British Legion during a march past of ex-servicemen, Colmore Row, 2nd July 1950.

Carnival beauty queen competitors, 1947.

THE BIRMINGHAM
ACCIDENT PREVENTION
COUNCIL

CERTIFICATE
OF MERIT
INFANTS

AWARDED TO *Thelma Jones.*

LORD MAYOR *JCBurman*

SECRETARY *D.M. Harbage*   CHAIRMAN *Wenmanebrook*

1948

How to get your new Ration Book

WHERE TO GO IN BIRMINGHAM
WHEN: 7th JUNE to 3rd JULY, 1948
HOURS: MONDAYS TO FRIDAYS ... 9 a.m. till 6.30 p.m.
SATURDAYS .... 9 a.m. till 4.0 p.m.

WEEK 3: 21st JUNE to 26th JUNE, 1948
Alphabetical Letters of Surname: K, L, M, N, O, P, Q, and R.

Centre No.	District	DISTRIBUTION CENTRE
1	CITY	Town Hall (Basement)
2	ASTON	Baptist Church, Yates Street
3	BALSALL HEATH	Friends' Institute, Oughton Rd., Moseley
4	ERDINGTON	Church Hall, Slade Road
5	HANDSWORTH	St. Peter's Hall, Arthur Road
6	HARBORNE	Harborne Baths
7	KING'S HEATH	King's Heath Baths, Institute Road
8	KINGSTANDING	Kingstanding Baths, Warren Farm Road
9	LADYWOOD	Methodist Church Hall, Monument Road
10	LEA HALL	Community Hall, Glebe Farm Road
11	NORTHFIELD	Northfield Baths, Bristol Road South
12	SALTLEY	Saltley Baths
13	SMALL HEATH	St. Giles' Institute, Green Lane
14	HALL GREEN	Methodist Church, York Road
15	WINSON GREEN	St. Cuthbert's Hall, Heath Street
16	YARDLEY	Church Road School

Any person who attends a Distribution Centre may collect Ration Books for others outside the alphabetical range allotted for the day.
Every effort should be made to call on the days allotted to the particular letter to avoid queues and congestion.
Factories, Firms and large Organisations may, as in previous years, participate in the "Block Scheme" by arranging in writing direct with the Food Executive Officer. All envelopes should be marked at the top left-hand corner: "Block Scheme."

1953, July 6: A memorable page in Birmingham's history was turned [on Saturday] when, after nearly 80 years' service to the city, the tramway undertaking closed. With appropriate ceremony, the last tram made its final run from the city terminus in Steelhouse Lane to Erdington and then passed to its last depot — the breaker' yard. To-day Birmingham is a city of buses.

Sweeter Times
Northfield Edition   1953

SUGAR OFF RATION
thanks to Conservatives

ON 27th SEPTEMBER SUGAR WAS DE-RATIONED. THE 13-YEAR RESTRICTION ON ITS SALE IS ENDED. WITH IT HAS GONE ONE OF THE HOUSEWIFE'S BIGGEST GRUMBLES.

This welcome "sweetener" comes as something of a present to the nation at the time of the Conservative Government's second "birthday."

In those two years a wholesale transformation has taken place in the food situation. Supplies are far more plentiful. There is a much wider variety of choice — and rationing is on its way out.

It's "sweeter times" all round—thanks to the Conservatives.

EVERYONE BENEFITS
The end of sugar rationing means much more than an extra lump in tea for the sweet-tooth.

It will be a tremendous help to the housewife. A number of food industries will be assisted. There will be more and better cakes, a wider variety of sweets and chocolate. A million less Government forms will be needed, and the taxpayers will be saved £200,000. Everyone will benefit as life becomes sweeter.

Just Think . .
If you are a housewife and were married since 1940, this is the first time in your married life you have been able to buy sugar as you like.
No child under 13 has lived in a period when sugar was not rationed. Thank the Conservatives for the change.

Flashback
The Socialists said they would nationalise the sugar industry. Thank goodness they didn't get the chance. Remember what Mr. Arthur Deakin said at the T.U.C. Congress this year : "One of the questions people ask about nationalisation is : 'What have we got out of it except higher prices ? '"

Sweeter Times for the Sweets !

Councillor Clem Sweet, Prospective Conservative Parliamentary Candidate for Northfield, helps himself to "an extra lump." Mrs. Sweet can make more cakes, while 8-year old Jennifer smiles happily at the thought of new lines at the sweet shop.

Printed by J. Goodman & Sons (Printers) Ltd., Cardigan Street, Birmingham, 4.   Published by the Birmingham Conservative Association, Birmingham, 3.

James Watt's statue in Ratcliff Place provides a vantage point during the Coronation Parade, (Queen Elizabeth II and Prince Philip) 7th June 1953.

Coronation Day in Fallowfield Avenue, Hall Green, 1953.

Coronation Concert, St Benedicts Road School, Small Heath, 1953. This is the first public appearance of Alton, (back right) who produced the show!

Nigel Road, Washwood Heath, Coronation Day, 1953.

The City Engineer and Surveyor, Sir Herbert Manzoni, points out features of the proposed Inner Ring Road Scheme to delegates from the Dublin City Council, who came to Birmingham to study slum clearance and redevelopment problems, 19th April 1955.

The Lord Mayor, Ald. Gibson, shakes hands with Marshal Bulganin at Elmdon, 23rd 1956. Behind the Marshal is Nikita Khrushchev.

Unveiling of the Boulton-Watt-Murdoch Memorial, Broad Street, 14th September 1956. The ceremony was performed by Sir Perry Mills, chairman of W & T Avery Ltd., the Soho Foundry that Boulton established in 1761.

SANT SINGH Shattar, of Bracebridge Street, Aston, had the distinction of becoming the first postman in Britain to be allowed to wear a turban on duty.

Six-foot-two with an impressive beard, he had his brass Post Office badge clipped to the front of his pale blue turban as he strode off on his rounds.

He spent five years as a factory machinist when he first came to Britain because his friends told him the Post Office would never tolerate a turban and a beard. *1960*

New car park... *1956*

BIRMINGHAM'S first multi-storey car park, built at a cost of £50,000, was opened in Cornwall Street on May 7.

The charge: four shillings a day.

The staff of The Motor Union Insurance Co. Ltd., Cherry Street, watch as their Branch Manager, Ronald Botteley, presents retirement gifts to Chief Cashier, Miss Ethel Mitchell, 1958. Moving to Temple Street in 1963, the company eventually became part of the Guardian Royal Exchange Group.

The Digbeth Flyover opens, 15th October 1961. It was built in one weekend and was originally known as a "carbridge".

Jewellers' Banquet, Grand Hotel, 20th January 1962.

The Lord Mayor, Ald. Ernest Horton, opens Birmingham Hospitals Broadcasting Network, 19th November 1962. These studios were in the MEB premises, Dale End, moving to Edgbaston in 1962 and to Dudley Road Hospital in 1988 - and all due to the generosity of industry and the public.

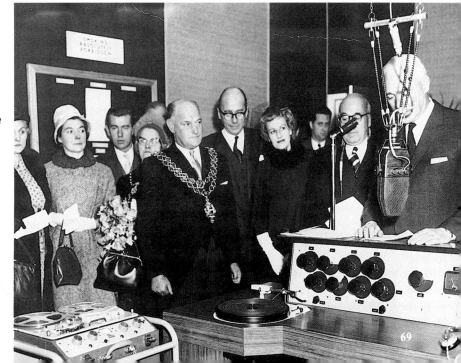

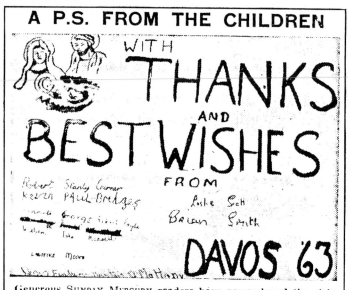

A P.S. FROM THE CHILDREN

WITH **THANKS** AND **BEST WISHES** FROM

Robert Stanley Cramer
Keith PAUL Bridges
Ashe Scott
George Brian Smith

DAVOS '63

Generous SUNDAY MERCURY readers have remembered the sick children this Christmas—and the children have not forgotten those who help them. Six of those signing this Christmas card to all helpers of the 'Give A Girl Health' Fund and Birmingham Branch of the British Red Cross Society are the boys sent to Switzerland by the Fund in September.

BERROW COURT HOTEL
WESTFIELD ROAD, EDGBASTON
BIRMINGHAM, 15
TELEPHONE: EDG. 1488 & 3289

R. G. Wilks, Esq.,
359, Rednal Road,
Kings Norton.
Birmingham. 141   16th. December. 1964.

Wedding Reception.
12.12.64.
=========

97 guests @ 15/-	£72.15.	0d.
15% service charge	10.18.	3d.
Room charge	15.15.	0d.
14 bottles Champagne	19. 5.	0d.
29 bottles White Bordeaux	15. 4.	6d.
6 bottles med. sherry	5. 5.	0d.
6 bottles dry sherry	5. 8.	0d.
75 Britvic fruit juices	4.13.	9d.
Service charge on 55 bottles	13.15.	0d.
	£162.19.	6d.

Paid with thanks,
R. Sargent-Thomas
30th. December. 1964.
BERROW COURT

Uniformed traffic wardens on the streets for the first time, 20th May 1963. The wardens were paired off with police constables to get general experience of the meter areas, as part of their training. Their first duties began in June.

BIRMINGHAM introduced a new rush-hour express bus service in April, 1967 — the Bristol Road "flier."
It whisked commuters from Birmingham to Rubery — or vice-versa — in a target scheduled time of 25 minutes.
This compared with 40 to 45 minutes for the ordinary service double-deckers.
The express service was a 54-seater one-man operated single-decker.

It's a tall order preparing for the opening of the Birmingham Zoo, Cannon Hill Park, 22nd April 1964. It is now known as the Birmingham Nature Centre.

Margot Bryant (Minnie Caldwell from "Coronation Street") cuts the tape to open the new shopping precinct at Perry Barr, 28th February 1964.

The boys of the 1st Handsworth Wood Cub Scouts Pack meet Sir Learie Constantine, MBE, July 1967. Sir Learie was, amongst other things, a superb West Indian cricketer, an author, broadcaster, barrister, High Commisioner for Trinidad and Tobago and a Governor of the BBC!

THE FIRST tenant of Chelmsley Wood new town looked round her new home on December 16, 1966.

She was Mrs. Patricia Hitchcock (left with son Gordon) who, with her husband, Stanley, and three sons, were pioneers among 15,000 families who were eventually to make up the new community.

"I'm delighted," said Mrs. Hitchcock, "It is the type of house I have always dreamed of having.

The Hitchcock's weekly rent was £4 9s. 6d. a week.

The 4,000th home at Chelmsley Wood is marked by the planting of a lime tree by Ald. Anthony Beaumont-Dark and other members of the Housing Committee, 6th November 1968. Mr Beaumont-Dark became the MP for Selly Oak in 1979.

A champagne opening for the £13,000,000 Aston Expressway, 1st May 1972. Coun. Harold Edwards (centre) and members of the Public Works Committee drink to its success.

The topping-out ceremony at the Alpha Tower is performed by the Lord Mayor, Ald. Vic Turton, 4th May 1972.

72

W.R.V.S. seek MEN members

14·APR·1971

Evening Mail Reporter

BIRMINGHAM'S Women's Royal Voluntary Service is out to attract men.

And to encourage them they have produced a special tie with the W.R.V.S. emblem woven into the design.

Miss Rhona Lamb, the Midlands Regional Organiser, said today: "We want the men to become members of W.R.V.S.

"We already have a few and their services as administrators, and in the running of the meals-on-wheels, books-on-wheels and general helpers services are invaluable," she said.

When men join they have to undergo the same training as the ladies, which includes talks on the service and a minimum of 60 hours' voluntary work.

'EMPLOYED'

"Then they get their member-ship badge or the special tie, just as they prefer," said Miss Lamb.

A W.R.V.S. spokeswoman in charge of meals-on-wheels in the city said the majority of men already "employed" were retired business people with time to spare.

She said: "Others are young working men who actually dash out from their jobs in the lunch-times and help us deliver meals.

"Nearly all the men seem to make time to chat to the people we can help, which is an invaluable part of the service," she added.

Joseph Cohen, of the Synagogue Council, Singers Hill, lays the foundation stone of the nursery classroom at King David Nursery School, Alcester Road, Moseley, 14th October 1973. A large public ceremony was cancelled because of the Middle East War.

Harold Wilson, the Leader of the Opposition, (now Lord Wilson), unveils the plaque to commemorate the opening of Birmingham's new Central Library Complex, 12th January 1974.

President praises the NEC

Francois - Xavier Ortoli, President, Commission of the European Communities.

On behalf of the Commission of the European Communities I should like to congratulate the Birmingham City Council, the Chamber of Industry and Commerce, the National Exhibition Centre Limited, and all those who have made possible the creation of the National Exhibition Centre.

This, the first national centre of its kind to be opened in the United Kingdom, will undoubtedly play a major role in presenting the finest of British manufacturers to world markets at large.

It is indeed a tribute to the people of the Birmingham area that this new venture should be launched in their region.

If I may speak on behalf of Britain's partners in the European Community, we all wish every success to your new enterprise and faithfully hope that the International Spring Fair will fulfil the best expectations deserved of your initiative and imagination.

1976

Le Président·

The Lord Mayor's Procession in New Street, 4th June 1977.

The flags fly as Great Lucas Street, Hockley, celebrates the wedding of the Prince and Princess of Wales, 29th July 1981.

Botanical Gardens Members, along with Lord Mayor, Coun. Peter Hollingworth, celebrate the 150th anniversary of the Gardens, 9th July 1982.

A topping-out with a difference! A glass fibre dome, after being
blessed, was lifted to its position on top of the Birmingham
Central Mosque's new minaret, 7th November 1982. The Mosque
is in Belgrave Road, Balsall Heath.

The President of the European Commision, Jacques Delors, after
laying the foundation stone for the International Convention
Centre in Broad Street. With President Delors, centre, are, from
left, Coun. Neville Bosworth (Conservative Group Leader), the
Lord Mayor, Coun. Denis Martineau, Nicholas Ridley (the
Secretary of State for the Environment), David Gilroy Bevan
(MP for Yardley), the Lady Mayoress, and Coun. Dick Knowles
(Leader of the City Council), 31st October 1986.

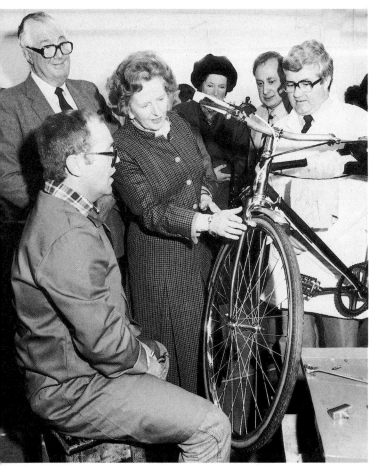

The Prime Minister, the Rt. Hon. Margaret Thatcher, admires the
work of blind students at Queen Alexandra College, Harborne,
9th January 1987.

During the centenary year of St John Ambulance a special
commemorative set of stamps was produced by the Post Office.
The set was officially launched at St John Ambulance
Headquarters, Lionel Street, in the presence of the Deputy Lord
Mayor and Lady Mayoress, Denis and Mollie Martineau and
representatives of St John Ambulance Brigade, 16th June 1987.

A party from Yardley Middle School, Warwick Road, Tyseley, presents a cheque to Beryl Romano, Appeals Manager of the Birmingham Dogs' Home, 14th December 1985.

NEW BARTHOLOMEW STREET

THE NEW BIRMINGHAM DOGS HOME

The model of The New Birmingham Dogs' Home, New Bartholomew Street, which opened on 26th October 1987, 95 years after the original Home opened.

City's RSPCA branch celebrates 125 years of service

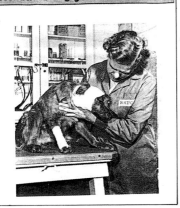

Brum's battle to care for our animals

EVENING MAIL TUESDAY, JULY 14, 1987

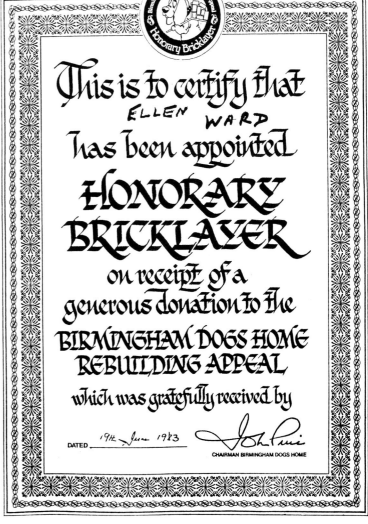

This is to certify that ELLEN WARD has been appointed HONORARY BRICKLAYER on receipt of a generous donation to the BIRMINGHAM DOGS HOME REBUILDING APPEAL which was gratefully received by

DATED 19th June 1983

CHAIRMAN BIRMINGHAM DOGS HOME

Sir Richard Attenborough hands over the keys of his wife's Daimler (with her permission of course!) to Alexander Patrick, Chairman of PMG Investments, for display in the Patrick Collection, Lifford Lane, Kings Norton, 12th January 1988. The Collection (a motor museum complex) is the family's permanent Centenary contribution to the City's infrastructure. In 1889 Joseph Patrick came to Birmingham, in the 1920's he was Chairman of the Brittanic Assurance Company and in 1930 his son Albert and grandson Joseph founded Patrick Motors.

TV personality Rustie Lee preparing to serve a knock-out meal to Muhammad Ali when he came to open the centre, in his name, in Hockley, August 1983. At the time, Rustie's restaurant was in Soho Hill, but today she delights her customers at her premises in Hurst Street.

Local comedian Don MacLean receives a cheque from pupils of Great Barr School, 20th July 1987. Don is a tireless worker for children's charities. Like Sid Field he was born in Sparkbrook.

THE HUB OF THE WHEEL

By 1956, Sir Herbert Manzoni, Birmingham City Engineer and Surveyor, had drawn up plans for a network of motorways based on a cartwheel design, around a central hub, its spokes running out to the boundaries of the city. Sir Herbert's planning would inevitably require the use of much steel and concrete, the creation of underpasses and flyovers and the utilisation of limited space, hence tower-blocks. In the Bull Ring area, the remarkable Rotunda and the revolutionary under-cover Shopping Centre, neither distinguished architecturally, have given good service over the years, but are due for replacement.

The excellent work done to focus attention on Victoria Square and Chamberlain Square has borne fruit for it is now possible to stay safely clear of most of the traffic to admire the view - and there is much to admire: an Italianate Council House with its compatible extension, the Museum and Art Gallery and a Parthenon-like Town Hall. Proceeding along Colmore Row one can find some fine Victorian banks. At the New Street end of Joseph Chamberlain's Corporation Street, if the eye gazes upwards, a number of examples of pleasing architecture with enduring qualities are revealed. Near at hand are the Victoria Law Courts, completed in 1891, which remain an excellent example of brick and terracotta, so resistant to grime and decay.

Returning to Paradise Street by way of New Street, we find the attractive facade of Queen's College preserved, disguising the modern offices behind. Paradise Street once contained the rounded Midland Institute, which was linked to the old Central Library in Ratcliff Place, but now forms part of Paradise Circus and Chamberlain Square where the new Central Library stands, an angular building in contrast to its companions but which houses one of the finest libraries in the land, staffed by the most delightful and helpful of people.

Recent years have brought us so much more to enjoy. The beautifully renovated Great Western Arcade is a delight for locals and tourists alike, and we can shop with ease and comfort in the wholly practical Pallasades, the futuristic Pavilions and in the latest of Birmingham's shopping centres, the City Plaza, in Cannon Street.

It has been said that Birmingham's motto "Forward" should be "Forward and Upward", so much new building having gone sky-high, but no matter what changes may yet come, somehow the starlings will still be around and Birmingham will continue to be its superb self.

The Bull Ring, seen from St Martin's Church, a typical fifties scene.

79

The Market Hall, showing some of the redevelopment under way, 29th August 1961.

Market Hall interior, June 1936.

...oor Street/Bull Ring, with Moor Street Station on ...e extreme left, 7th August 1955.

Queuing for seaside tickets? Moor Street Station, 15th June 1962.

Curzon Street Station, seen here in 1938, was the first railway station in Birmingham, and the terminal for Robert Stephenson's London and Birmingham Railway Line. In 1988 it finds itself, in its 150th year, renovated and housing Task Undertakings Ltd. (a charitable company providing employment and training opportunitites).

81

The Beehive, Albert Street, 29th May 1953. An application had been made to the Architects Dept. to place a sign where the arrow indicates.

The Rotunda, in its early stages of construction, 2nd June 1962. It was completed two years later.

Bull Street, 1889.

Evening Despatch, Friday, April 18, 1958.

Lewis's from Bull Street, 19th July 1955.

Corporation Street, with Lewis's on the right, 1938.

Kings Hall Market and the Grand Casino, Corporation Street, 30th May 1961.

Kings Hall Market

CORPORATION STREET (Opp. Old Square)

'For the Finest Values in Town'

1958

HALL 1 AND BALCONY

KEYCUTTING AND ENGRAVING. Service while you wait. Stand 1.

LADIES' BLOUSES. "Drip Dry," most colours and styles. Stand 24. 14/11 ea.

REGENCY STRIPE. 36in. and 48in. wide to match. Large selection. Stand 11. 36in. wide. 3/11 yd.

'LETTE SHEETS. Full size, excellent quality, special reduction. Stand 17. 19/11 pair.

FLORAL CRETONNE. 48in. wide, attractive colours, bargain offer. Stand 9. 2/3 yd.

HANDBAGS AND SHOPPING BAGS, at rock bottom prices. Stand 4. Ex.: Large Vanity Cases. 8/6 each.

WALLPAPER. Crown, a wonderful selection, special bargain offer. Stand 22 1/11 roll.

BROCADE, 48in. wide, lovely curtaining, colours to choose. Stand 16. 4/6 yd.

TAFFETA, 36in. wide. Net, 54in. wide, to match, beautiful colours. Stand 20. 2/- yd.

RHODIA VOILE, 36in. wide, frilled, full range of colours to choose. Stand 10. 4/6 yd.

WATCH AND CLOCK REPAIRS. Watch glasses fitted while you wait. Stand 35. From 2/- each.

FLOCK NYLON, 36in. wide, super quality, lovely colours to choose. Stand 19. 6/11 yd.

TERYLENE AND VOILE NET, 36in. wide, frilled, finest selection of colours to choose. Stand 14. 3/11 yd.

BRIDAL WEAR a speciality. Fluorescent Nylon Net, 54in. wide, in 12 colours. Stand 2. 4/6 yd.

REGENCY STRIPE, 48in. wide, 4 attractive colours to choose. Stand 18. 4/6 yd.

PAINT AND DISTEMPER. All the leading makes now in stock. Stand 21. Reasonable Prices.

ONE-MINUTE Keycutting and Engraving service, the quickest service in town. Stand 1A.

WATCHES AND CLOCKS. Canteens at lowest possible prices. Stand 6. Ex.: Watches, guaranteed, 35/- each.

FRILLED NET, 48in. and 52in. wide. Pink, white, cream, spot. Stand 2. 36in. wide. 3/6 yd.

DRESS NET, 54in. wide, 36in. Taffeta to match. Latest colours. Stand 23. 2/- yd.

ORIENTAL SLIPPERS AND HAND-BAGS, all hand made, gay exciting colours. Stand 34. Slippers 18/11 pr.

JEWELLERY. All the latest designs in Necklets, Brooches and Earrings. Stand 7. Ex.: Silver Marcasite Rings 10/- each.

MOQUETTE. UNCUT, 52in./54in. wide, special bargain offer to clear. Stand 5. 8/11 yd.

DRESS MATERIALS. 36in. wide, ideal for Summer Dresses, special reduction. Stand 12. 2/11 yd.

TAPESTRY, 50in. wide, rich attractive colours to choose. Stand 15. 6/6 yd.

CANDLEWICK BEDSPREADS, 90in. x 100in. Lifetime use, modern designs. Stand 13. 29/11 each.

GIRLS' HANDBAGS, in latest Pastel Shades. Special offer. Stand 8. 6/11 ea.

HALL 2

CRETONNE. 48in. wide, very heavy quality. 3 attractive shades to choose. Stand 38. 3/6 yd.

GLAZED COTTON, 36in. wide, Spotted, in 4 colours. Stand 36. 2/6 yd.

TERYLENE NET, 48in. wide, Cream, beige and white, nice quality. Stand 49. 4/11 yd.

COTTON PIQUE, 36in. wide, Floral and Stripe, special reduction. Stand 47. 3/6 yd.

MOQUETTE. UNCUT, 54in. wide, wonderful quality, patterns to choose. Stand 42. 8/6 yd.

PIQUE, 36in. wide. Spotted, in 5 attractive shades. Stand 37. 3/6 yd.

DRESS CANDY STRIPE, 36in. wide, very latest shades. Stand 41. 2/- yd.

BRIDES' AND BRIDESMAIDS' WEAR a speciality. Net, Lace and Taffeta to match. Stand 43. Flock Nylon, 36in. wide, 7/6 yd.

CRETONNE. 48in. wide, lovely Floral design, 4 colours to choose. Stand 48. 3/6 yd.

FURNISHINGS. Regency Stripe, 36in. and 48in. wide to match. Stand 44. 4/6 yd.

POPLIN, 36in. wide, "Sanforized Shrunk" in attractive shades. Bargain offer. Stand 46. 2/11 yd.

BRIDES' AND BRIDESMAIDS' WEAR a speciality. Dress Net, Lace and Taffeta to match. Poult Taffeta, 36in. wide. 3/6 yd.

CRETONNE, 36in. wide, for Curtaining, many shades and designs. Stand 45. 1/11 yd.

CRETONNE, 48in. wide, "Silver Glint" heavy quality. Stand 40. 3/6 yd.

MOQUETTE. UNCUT, 52/54in. wide. Spot design, nice quality. Stand 39. 8/6 yd.

One-way Traffic

1933, June 6: A one-way traffic scheme for the centre of Birmingham came into operation yesterday.

1947, January 29: There were further heavy falls of snow in Birmingham yesterday. Temperatures were down to 20 degrees.

1947, February 3: Snow fell in Birmingham yesterday from early morning until late afternoon.

1947, February 5: Britain was swept by blizzards yesterday. Midland roads were blocked and villages cut off. Birmingham Public Works Department cleared 500 tons of snow in the night.

1947, February 10: Fog shrouded Birmingham. The snowfall during the week-end was 2 to 3 inches. The temperature rose to 30 degrees.

[In 18 days a million tons of snow fell on Birmingham of which about 30,000 tons were removed by the Corporation and contractors.]

The Central Fire Station, July 1946.

Moland Street/Aston Street, 1938. This is now the site of Aston University.

General Hospital, Steelhouse Lane, shortly after it opened in 1897.

Children's Surgical Ward, General Hospital, c. 1900. The ward was furnished by teachers and pupils of King Edward VI High School.

Steelhouse Lane, c. 1947.

The Wesleyan & General, with the Gaumont Cinema on our right, 22nd September 1965. These buildings have recently been demolished.

The Haberdashery Dept., Edward Grey's, Bull Street, c. 1900.

Snow Hill, 1899.

"The Cornishman" waits to start its journey, Snow Hill Station, 30th July 1960.

From the "Birmingham Weekly Post," February 15, 1902

"FORWARD" can still be claimed as Birmingham's motto. The City Gas Department are experimenting with a new gas lamp, which they have erected at the corner of Livery Street and Colmore Row. It throws out a flood of light equal to 700 candlepower, double the power of any incandescent street light at present in the city. Waiting passengers for the trams will now be able to read their newspapers whilst standing in the queue, the light being so brilliant. General comment has been made on the experiment and hopes are expressed that further lamps of the same power will soon be seen in other important parts of the city.

Colmore Row, 1960.

Lunch hour in St Philip's churchyard, June 1960.

St Philip's Cathedral, October 1973.

"BIG BRUM"

Local people take as much notice of their "Big Brum," which keeps them up to time, as do Londoners of their "Big Ben." The latter, it is true, strikes affectionately at the heart of the Commonwealth, but to the natives of the Second City there is more than a sneaking regard for their Council House Clock as it is officially designated. "Big Brum," made by Gillet & Co., of Croydon was presented to the city in 1885 by Mr. A. Follet Osler. The pendulum is 15 ft. long and weighs 4 cwt.; the dials are each 10½ feet in diameter; the hour bell weighs 3 tons 6 cwts. and is struck by a 180lb. hammer; and quarter bells range in weight from 12 cwt. to 2 tons 2 cwt. The height of the clock tower is 153 ft. 4 inches.

In 1958 the movement was overhauled and mechanism installed for automatically raising the timekeeping weight and operating the chiming and striking sections, so removing the need for manual winding which was previously necessary four times each week.

The Council House extension, Congreve Street/Edmund Street, 1911. The arched bridge links it to the Museum and Art Gallery.

Chamberlain Place, 27th March 1954. This was how it appeared after the alterations for the Festival of Britain, 1951. In 1980 further reconstruction took place.

TWO GUINEAS REWARD

Will be paid to anyone who can give Information which will lead to the Conviction of the person who threw a cast-iron Cannon Ball, about 4lbs. weight, through one of the Edmund Street Windows of the Library, about 11-15 p.m. on the night of Thursday, the 13th October.

By order of the Free Libraries Committee,

J. D. MULLINS,
Chief Librarian.

The old Central Library, Ratcliff Place, 16th March 1953.

"Big Brum" seems to be dwarfed by cranes as the new Central Library begins to take its place in the Paradise Circus scheme, 20th September 1969.

Gas Street Basin, 11th February 1969.

Panoramic view showing the site of the International Convention Centre (right of the Crown clock tower), Broad Street, 16th February 1986.

Work begins on Birmingham's prestigious International Convention Centre, due for completion in 1991. The picture, taken from Cambridge Street, shows Baskerville House on the extreme left, 3rd May 1988.

From the Horse Fair with a tram emerging from Holloway Head on the left. The policeman controls the cars driving away up Suffolk Street. A tram approaches along John Bright Street, c. 1946.

Friday's best 3 pennyworth

BIRMINGHAM **Weekly Post** and MIDLAND PICTORIAL

1956

Bristol Street/Little Bow Street, with the site of the present Dome on the left, 4th July 1957.

From Worcester Street, looking down Station Street towards Hill Street, 1946.

94

The last bus to use the bridge at Hill Street for two years, 28th February 1949. All through traffic used the temporary bridge.

Read all about it! Hill Street end of Queen's Drive, 24th April 1964.

Hill Street, with New Street Station prior to modernisation, 3rd October 1962.

Paradise Street, c. 1895.

96

Victoria Square. When Christ Church was demolished in 1899, it was replaced by Christ Church Buildings, generally known as Galloway's Corner, here seen on the left in June 1932. This was, in turn, demolished in 1970. By coincidence, the stone for the General Post Office (on the right) was laid the year the city was granted its charter.

Christt Church Passage, looking up from New Street to Waterloo Street, 3rd December 1969.

New Street, 24th November 1952.

Cannon Street from New Street, June 1892.

New Street, looking towards the Town Hall, from Corporation Street, c. 1890.

New Street, with Worcester Street on the left, c. 1904.

King Edward VI Grammar School, New Street, c. 1934. This was demolished and on the left-hand side of the site the Paramount Cinema opened in September 1937. It became the Odeon after the war.

Corporation Street, 10th April 1961.

Fore Street/Corporation Street, 21st September 1960.

Martineau Street, 21st March 1951.

*Football fans queue in Martineau Street, October
1937.*

When tea was 8s. a pound

100 YEARS OF BARROW'S

by a special correspondent

IN those old days when coaches lurched and rattled over Birmingham's unpaved streets—and were occasionally overturned on piles of stones in the road—Samuel Galton of Dudson (Duddeston), a Quaker gunmaker, walked into a coffee warehouse in Bull-street to do a little shopping.

He bought: 3lb. Souchong tea at 8s. a pound and 6lb. fine coffee at 3s. 4d. a pound and having paid over the lordly sum of £2 4s. Sam Galton ceased to be of historical interest, retreating once more into that odd private life of his in which he practised the belief of a Quaker and the trade of a gunsmith.

But with scratching quill Sam's purchases were faithfully entered in the new ledger of the equally new coffee shop. It was the first entry.

"Sink or Swim"

Possibly the attention of this first customer had been attracted by an advertisement in "Aris's Gazette," in which 23-year-old John Cadbury, "Tea dealer and coffee roaster," had in small type and with much courtesy offered his wares.

That was in 1824. John Cadbury, opening his tea warehouse at 93, Bull-street, next door to the family textile business, was told bluntly by his father to "sink or swim." Old R. T. Cadbury (known in Quaker circles as "King Richard") would be pleasantly surprised at his son's commercial buoyancy if he were alive today.

He worked hard to make his business a success.

In his spare time he began to experiment with the grinding of cocoa beans with a pestle and mortar. In 1831 he rented premises in nearby Crooked-lane and began to roast and grind beans on a larger scale and to sell the product in the Bull-street shop.

Soon he wanted to give more time to this manufacture from which the great firm of Cadbury was to grow, so he suggested that his nephew, Richard Cadbury Barrow, should come to help him with the Bull-street business.

R. C. Barrow extended the range of commodities from tea and coffee to a much wider range of general groceries Later, as Birmingham developed, he sold the site of the Bull-street warehouse in order to facilitate the cutting of Corporation-street and he himself became one of the first leaseholders in the new street, where he built large new premises which he called Lancaster Buildings.

Changing face

In 1886 his son, Harrison Barrow, joined him in business, and when R. C. Barrow died in 1894 the business was formed into a private limited company with Harrison Barrow as managing-director.

Ald. Harrison Barrow, who this year retires from his distinguished life in municipal affairs, has been continuously associated with the business ever since he joined it as a boy of 18. And so, quite suddenly, we leave the history-book-world of dates and development and find ourselves among contemporaries.

Scarcely, it seems, has the quaint figure of Sam Galton left the counter with his Souchong tea and fine coffee than the post-war housewives of 1949 are there with their shopping baskets making similar purchases — though in slightly reduced quantities and at vastly reduced prices.

The 125th anniversary of Barrow's Stores, Corporation Street, 28th March 1949. George Turner serves Lord Mayor and Lady Mayoress, Coun. and Mrs John Burman.

THE RACKHAMS STORY

The retail drapers, Wilkinson & Riddell, who were established in 1851, and whose premises were at 78, Bull Street, took on two new sales assistants in 1861. One of these was John Rackham. Twenty years later John and his colleague William Matthews took over and extended the shop into Temple Row. It took the name of Rackhams.

The new Corporation Street was soon made and in 1898 Rackhams was extended into the North Western Arcade over the Snow Hill Tunnel. By 1918 the business had a fine new frontage in Bull Street; a pneumatic cash-tube system was installed in 1923 and their first motor-driven delivery van was purchased.

On the night of 26th October 1940 the store received a direct hit in a bombing raid and merchandise was blasted into the street. Through a hole in the floor trains could be seen passing along the tunnel beneath!

Harrods Ltd. bought Rackhams in 1955, having also purchased their present site. Work began in 1957 on an eight-phase project for a new department store, office tower-block and arcade. Rackhams moved into the completed Temple Row section in 1959, coinciding with the demolition of the old Bull Street shop. The new store was officially opened in November 1960 - nine months ahead of schedule.

Bull Street/Temple Row, showing the original Rackhams shop, 1958.

The Cobden Hotel awaits demolition, 1957.

Rackhams takes shape, 13th October 1959.

The City Centre, 1967.

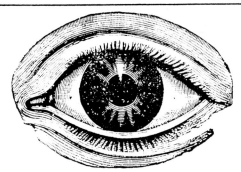

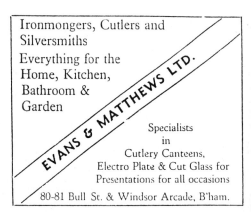

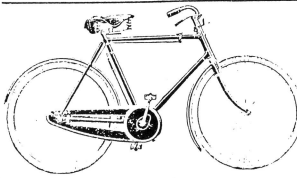

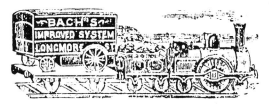

MODES OF TRANSPORT THEN AND NOW

1935

THINGS have moved in the world of transport during the last twenty-five years. You don't appreciate it until you come to glance through the news items of 1910.

On 3 January of that year, for instance, a serious trap accident took place at Alvechurch. Three people were watching the North Warwickshire Hunt from the trap, when the horse bolted, throwing them out. They all sustained serious injuries.

A few weeks later there was a sequel to a trotting match at Solihull Police Court, when three men were summoned for furious driving. It was alleged that the men were driving "gigs" along the Coventry-road, at Sheldon, at a speed of 16 to 18 miles an hour. One of the defendants indignantly denied that "his old crock" could do the pace alleged.

You remember the "Harborne Express," which made its last journey some months ago. Well, even that had its critics in 1910. A reader of the *Birmingham Gazette*, who signed himself "Punctual," sent the following protest to the editor: "I do not think that we could have more striking evidence in support of a tramway service to Harborne than that furnished by the 'Harborne Express,' which failed to run at its appointed time on Monday."

Great developments were beginning to take place in the aviation world at about this time, but flying was still a very hazardous occupation.

Addressing members of the Midland Aero Club in February Captain J. H. Cooke said he did not think they had yet reached the stage when the conquest of the air could be said to have been achieved. He did not think they could say they had got anything like a successful airship, neither would they have a successful airship until they had a machine which would enable a man to fly from place to place at any time and in all weathers, according to scheduled time.

SOME STRIKING 1910-35 COMPARISONS

	1910.		1935.
AREA OF BIRMINGHAM	13,477 acres	......	51,147 acres
POPULATION	525,960	......	1,028,000
HIGHWAYS (ADOPTED)	283 miles	......	813 miles
STREET LAMPS	14,485	......	39,848
MUNICIPAL HOUSES	164	......	41,518
HOUSES ERECTED BY PRIVATE ENTERPRISE FROM 1910 TO 1934	—	......	34,363
TOWN PLANNING:— Area of schemes approved	—	......	15,159 acres
Percentage of area of city in approved schemes	—	......	30%
In addition, the Birmingham (South-West) Scheme, covering 9,863 acres, is awaiting the approval of the Ministry of Health, and together with the other schemes in active preparation, brings the TOTAL AREA WITHIN THE CITY PLANNED, OR IN COURSE OF BEING PLANNED, to	—	......	38,504 acres
Percentage of the area of city in schemes approved and prepared or being prepared	—	......	75%

HERE AND THERE

Opening a coloured map of Birmingham, it is quite remarkable just how many areas of green there are, indicating the presence of parks, fields and woodlands. The view from the top windows of the Broadcasting Centre at Pebble Mill is a panorama of trees and parks. Office and residential tower-blocks are around, of course, as are busy roads and factory sites, but "green and pleasant" is still the overwhelming impression. Thanks to planned expansion and to the control of pollution, whole areas have been transformed. It is noteworthy that, quite recently, kingfishers, those most colourful British birds, have been spotted within 200 yards of Snow Hill Station. Birmingham has a commendable habit of being able to transform itself to the extent that even people born here and returning after, say, 10 to 15 years, hardly recognise some of the districts.

In the 19th century, industry close to the inner city drove the well-to-do out to live in Acocks Green and Moseley and later to Hagley, Solihull and Knowle. Edgbaston, however, was safe, as the Calthorpes, the owners of the estate, refused to allow the erection of factories and warehouses. Edgbaston became a shining example of town-planning and, despite its proximity to the city centre, it remains an attractive Regency and early-Victorian suburb, perhaps unsurpassed in any other British industrial city. The developments of Kingstanding, Weoley Castle, Fox Hollies, Gospel Farm and Billesley Farm in the 1930's and Castle Vale after the Second World War, have helped to make Birmingham the largest Housing Authority in the land. Birmingham, in the heart of England, will have a heart of oak to commemorate its 100 years as a city, with the planting of 100 English oaks on the River Rea walkway to the south of Cannon Hill Park. Mixed woodlands on 50 other sites form part of the project.

In 1951, the late Michael Rix, local lecturer and historian, hoped that Birmingham would "set an example by drawing up a revolutionary long-term plan for the nation's second city", and it seems that the city has more than fulfilled his hope.

Warwick Road, Acocks Green, 13th June 1939. The Dolphin is on the left.

Duddeston Mill Road/Adderley Road, Adderley Park, 29th July 1949.

Alum Rock Road, with the Capitol Cinema, on the right, 17th April 1957.

Aston Brook Street/Aston Road, 14th June 1951.

Gem Street School, Aston, 1896.

Lichfield Road, Aston, 12th November 1965.

Rear of 170 Belgrave Road, Balsall Heath, 25th June 1962.

Bordesley Green, mid-way between Blake Lane and Fifth Avenue, 26th April 1961.

Tramlines set in cobbles

The Birmingham Post

Coleshill Street, Dale End, with the Gaiety Picture House on the immediate left, c. 1946.

The Crown Inn, Deritend. c. 1900. probably Birmingham's oldest surviving building.

Hagley Road, Edgbaston, c. 1895.

High Street, Erdington, April 1928. An obviously educated dog reads the Melox advertisement!

No. 5 Court, Great Colmore Street, Five Ways, c. 1905.

Five Ways, from Hagley Road, 24th November 1960.

Soho Road, Handsworth, 1939.

The Dog Show, Handsworth Park, August 1962.

Robin Hood Island, Hall Green, 1955.

High Street, Harborne, 19th May 1953.

Hingeston Street, Hockley, 16th January 1958.

Viewed from Warstone Lane, Hockley (looking towards Vyse Street and Frederick Street) October 1954, we see the clock commemorating Joesph Chamberlain's visit to South Africa. He was then Secretary of State and the clock, unveiled by his wife Mary, on the 30th January 1904, was made by W.F. Evans & Sons of Soho Road.

The frontage to Kings Heath Station, Alcester Road, 22nd October 1962. Texas Homecare Ltd., is now on the site of the actual station.

Looking from Wharf Road towards Rednal Road, with Redditch Road on the left, Kings Norton, 16th May 1949.

120

Monument Road/Wood Street, Ladywood, 10th February 1959.

Barford Road Primary School, Ladywood, 6th March 1968.

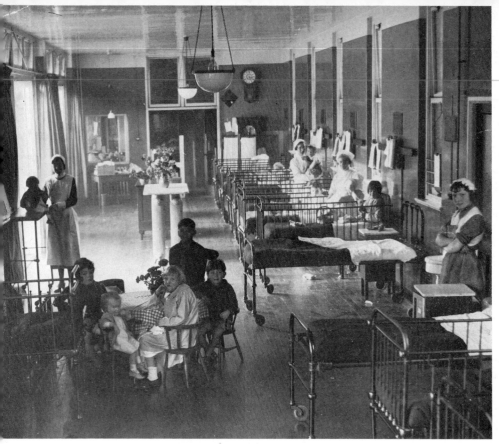

Children's Hospital, Ladywood, 15th October 1934.

Work in progress on the site of the Babies' Block at the Children's Hospital, 3rd September 1937.

Lozells Road, with St Paul's in the distance, 1960.

MR. CHAMBERLAIN'S MESSAGE

TO THE ELECTORS OF THE SEVEN DIVISIONS OF BIRMINGHAM:

"England expects Birmingham to be true to its past, and will not be disappointed.

"Where Birmingham leads, all England will follow."

J. Chamberlain

HIGHBURY, MOOR GREEN,
January 13th, 1910.

ted and Published by
DAY Ltd., Typs., Birmingham.

JULY 26, 1956

Because interest in speedway is declining, Birmingham Valuation Panel today reduced the rateable value of Birchfield Harrier's sports ground, race track and premises at Perry Barr from £900 to £750.

The club had suggested that the proper figure should be £550.

Council houses in Birmingham are being built at £1,530 for a two-bedroomed house and £1,680 for a three-bedroomed house, the city council reported. 1952

St Mary's Row, Moseley Village, 23rd June 1939.

Great Lister Street, Nechells, 23rd April 1959, just prior to demolition.

Brighton Place, New Summer Street, Newtown, c. 1905.

Leonard Seabourne, with his dog Bob, outside his cottage shop in Merritts Brook Lane, Northfield, 14th August 1952.

KEEPING IT IN THE FIRM

A REMARKABLE series of coincidences took place in the fog to-day.

A large Birmingham firm, which possesses its own fire brigade, received a summons to a house fire.

On the way the fire engine crashed into a lorry.

The coincidence was: that the lorry belonged to the same firm . . . the house to which the brigade were called also belonged to the firm—and is tenanted by a member of the firm's fire brigade!

The end of the oak tree from which Selly Oak derives its name. Oak Tree Lane, 1909.

Travelling out of the city along Bristol Road, Selly Oak, 12th March 1957.

Travelling out of the city along Bristol Road, Selly Oak, 12th March 1957.

Small Heath Library, Little Green Lane/Green Lane, 6th November 1973 (now Jame Masjid & Muslim Community Centre).

on all the best-laid tables

CAKES
and
BREAD
by

A.D.Wimbush & Son
BIRMINGHAM LTD.

Wedding, Christening, Birthday and all types of
Anniversary Cakes

DESIGNED AND MADE TO ORDER

A. D. WIMBUSH & SON LTD., Bakers, Caterers and Confectioners
Small Heath, Birmingham, 9.

Small Heath Park Pool, overlooking Tennyson Road, 20th May 1958.

127

Stoney Lane, Yardley, 1908.

Stechford Lane/Alum Rock Road, Ward End, 27th July 1959.

Children in need, c. 1900. NSPCC Inspectors have been at work protecting children in Birmingham since the year before the city was granted its charter. The NSPCC now has two fully operational Child Protection teams in Chelmsley Wood and West Heath.

Girl Guides preparing the camping site in Goodrest Lane, West Heath (now Kings Norton), 5th March 1966.

Ye Olde Swan, Washwood Heath, c. 1910.

Church Road, Yardley, 22nd June 1955.

Heath Street, Winson Green, 10th January 1958.

Winson Green Prison entrance, 20th August 1959.

The new entrance to Winson Green Prison, which stands just to the right of the old gates, 27th January 1988.

"Volunteer" the first Airliner to land at Elmdon, May 1939.

The Airport Committee of 1934 sanctioned a Municipal Airport at Elmdon, which was then a small flying school. The Duchess of Kent (who was later to become Princess Marina upon the death of her husband on RAF service) officially opens the airport on a very rainy day, 8th July 1939.

BRITISH EUROPEAN AIRWAYS
Air Terminal, Civic Centre, 1.
(Cen 8271—Bookings and Enquiries).
Telegrams: Bealine: 'Phone Birmingham.
Sales Officer (Midlands): T. G. Staddon.

Birmingham (Elmdon) Airport, 26.
(Enquiries—She 3158 ; Freight—She 2441, extn. 04).
Station Superintendent: R. W. Thairs.

An Air Terminal is opened next to the Civic Centre, by Lord Douglas of Kirtleside, 30th October 1951. The bus service, to and from the Airport, finished on 5th January 1963.

MARCH 1988

AIRPORT SET TO DOUBLE

A £35 MILLION expansion plan has been hailed as the first step in moves to double the capacity at Birmingham International Airport by the year 2000.

The three-year programme was announced at the end of January as figures showed a 25% leap in the number of passengers with more than 2.7 million expected to have used the airport by the end of the current financial year in March, a level planners did not predict would be reached until 1990.

It is now predicted demand will reach six million passengers by the end of the century.

Cargo freights handled have also jumped 50% to 26,700 tonnes this year.

It is expected to make nearly £2 million profit this current year instead of a predicted loss.

The expansion programme includes £11 million on improving the passenger terminal, extending the building to cater for an extra million people a year. More lounge space, baggage handling facilities and an expanded check-in area as well as more shopping and catering facilities are also included in the plans.

Another £6 million will go on expanding the cargo handling operation which is expected to grow by a further 60% over the next two years.

The enlarged, modernised Birmingham International Airport, opened by the Queen and the Duke of Edinburgh, 30th May 1984. Amongst those acting as hosts were Coun. Beardwood, Chairman of the Airport Committee and Airport

134

ACKNOWLEDGEMENTS

(for providing photographs, for encouragement and numerous other favours)

Neil Allen; Stanley Arnold (Arnold's Stores); Automobile Association; Patrick Baird; George Bartram Press Relations; BBC in the Midlands; Birmingham City Council; Birmingham Dog Show; Birmingham Hospitals Broadcasting Network; Birmingham Midland Institute and Conference Centre; Birmingham Post and Mail Staff; Birmingham Reference Library, Local Studies; Birmingham Women's Cricket Club; Nell Blackburn; Sally Bloxsidge; Botanical Gardens; Boys' Brigade; Braidwood School for the Deaf; British Red Cross; BRMB Radio; Peter Brookes; Betty Buckley; Cadbury Schweppes Ltd.; Kath and Dave Carpenter; Central Independent TV plc; City of Birmingham Development Department; Jean Clements; Firmin & Sons plc; Judith Foster; Girl Guides' Association; Cedric Green; Avril Guest; Gladys Guise; Clive Hardy; H.M. Prison, Winson Green; Beryl Holland; John Holland; Robert Holmes; Anne Jennings; Thelma and David Jones; Peter Jones; Malcolm Keeley (Midland Bus & Transport Museum, Wythall); Ken Kelly; Jock Kilgour; Kings Heath Hockey Club; Gladys Ling; Lord Mayor, Coun. Harold Blumenthal; Lord Mayor's Parlour; Peter Mearns; Midland Association of Restaurants, Caterers and Hotels; Sheila Moore; The New Birmingham Dogs' Home; N.S.P.C.C.; John O' Keefe; Patrick Collection; Andrew Peet; Olive and Joe Pocius; David Pond; William Powell & Sons (Gunmakers) Ltd.; Gwen and Maurice Price; Victor J. Price; Railway Correspondence and Travel Society, West Midlands; Hilda Rees; Remploy Ltd.; Jill Robinson; Joe Russell; R.S.P.C.A.; St John Ambulance; Salvation Army; Selly Oak Rugby Football Club; Seymour Hardy Partnership; Murray Smith; Gordon Stretch; Task Undertakings Ltd.; Betty Teague; Brian Thompson; TSB Bank; Jean and Vic Turton; Andy Wade; Ellen Ward; June and Albert Watkins; West Midlands Fire Service; Joan and Bob Wilkes; Rosemary Wilkes; Lottie Williams; Norman Worwood; W.R.V.S.

Please forgive any possible omissions. Every effort has been made to include all organisations and individuals involved in the book.

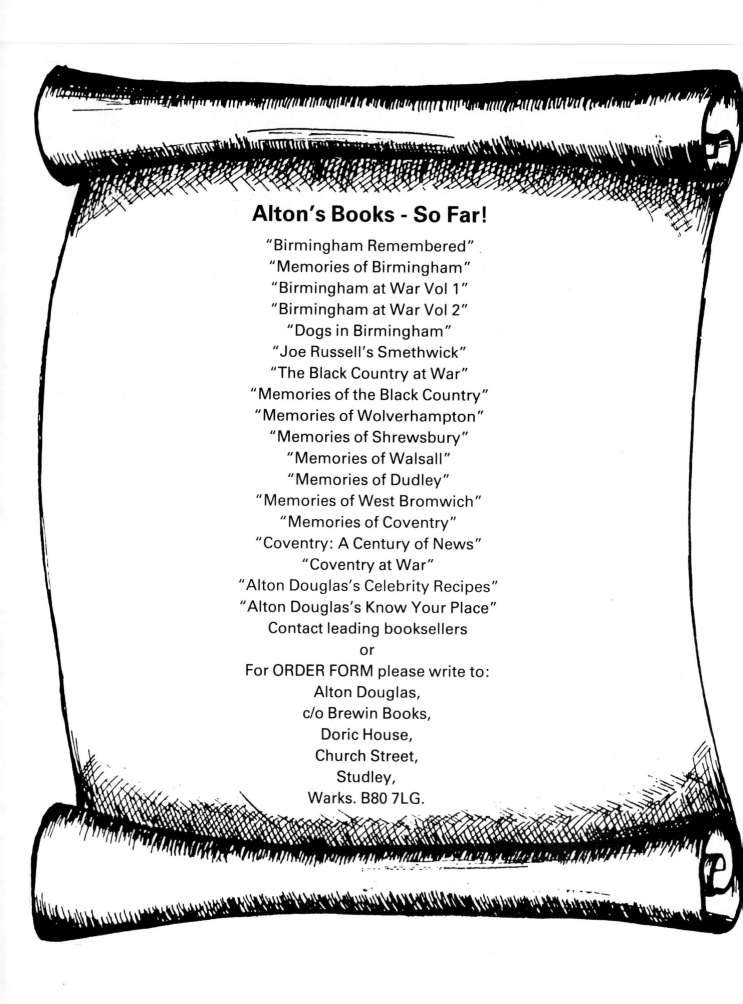

Alton's Books - So Far!

"Birmingham Remembered"
"Memories of Birmingham"
"Birmingham at War Vol 1"
"Birmingham at War Vol 2"
"Dogs in Birmingham"
"Joe Russell's Smethwick"
"The Black Country at War"
"Memories of the Black Country"
"Memories of Wolverhampton"
"Memories of Shrewsbury"
"Memories of Walsall"
"Memories of Dudley"
"Memories of West Bromwich"
"Memories of Coventry"
"Coventry: A Century of News"
"Coventry at War"
"Alton Douglas's Celebrity Recipes"
"Alton Douglas's Know Your Place"
Contact leading booksellers
or
For ORDER FORM please write to:
Alton Douglas,
c/o Brewin Books,
Doric House,
Church Street,
Studley,
Warks. B80 7LG.

The City Centre as it would have looked in 1889.